The *Journal of the History of Philosophy* Monograph Series
Edited by Richard A. Watson and Charles M. Young

Also in this series

Aristotle on the Many Senses of Priority
John J. Cleary

Kant's Newtonian Revolution in Philosophy
Robert Hahn

The Scottish Enlightenment and the Theory of Spontaneous Order
Ronald Hamowy

Shūzō Kuki and Jean-Paul Sartre: Influence and Counter-Influence in the Early History of Existential Phenomenology
Stephen Light

John Craige's "Mathematical Principles of Christian Theology"
Richard Nash

The Dream of Descartes
Gregor Sebba

The Philosophical Orations of Thomas Reid
D. D. Todd

Epistemology and Skepticism: An Enquiry into the Nature of Epistemology
George Chatalian

Descartes on Seeing: Epistemology and Visual Perception
Celia Wolf-Devine

"Infini Rien"
Pascal's Wager and the Human Paradox

Leslie Armour

Published for
The Journal of the History of Philosophy, Inc.

SOUTHERN ILLINOIS UNIVERSITY PRESS
Carbondale and Edwardsville

Library of Congress Cataloging-in-Publication Data

Armour, Leslie, 1931–
"Infini rien" : Pascal's wager and the human paradox / Leslie Armour.
p. cm. — (The Journal of the history of philosophy monograph series)
Includes bibliographical references and index.
1. Pascal, Blaise, 1623–1662. Pensées. 2. God—Proof—History of
doctrines. 3. Pascal, Blaise, 1623–1662—Knowledge—Neoplatonism.
4. Neoplatonism. I. Title. II. Series.
B1904.G63A76   1993
230'.2—dc20   92-27762
ISBN 0-8093-1839-3   CIP

CONTENTS

THE *JOURNAL OF THE HISTORY OF PHILOSOPHY*
Monograph Series

THE *JOURNAL OF THE HISTORY OF PHILOSOPHY* MONOGRAPH SERIES, CON-
sisting of volumes averaging 80 to 120 pages, accommodates serious studies in
the history of philosophy that are between article length and standard book size.
Editors of learned journals have usually been able to publish such studies only
by truncating them or by publishing them in sections. In this series, the *Journal
of the History of Philosophy* presents, in volumes published by Southern Illinois
University Press, such works in their entirety.

The historical range of the *Journal of the History of Philosophy* Monograph
Series is the same as that of the *Journal* itself—from ancient Greek philosophy to
the twentieth century. The series includes extended studies on given philosophers,
ideas, and concepts; analyses of texts and controversies; new translations and
commentaries on them; and new documentary findings about various thinkers
and events in the history of philosophy.

The editors of the Monograph Series, the directors of the *Journal of the History
of Philosophy,* and other qualified scholars evaluate submitted manuscripts. Those
manuscripts concerning ancient and medieval philosophy should be sent to Professor Charles M. Young, Department of Philosophy, Claremont Graduate School,
Claremont, CA 91711. Manuscripts on modern and recent philosophy should be
sent to Professor Richard A. Watson, Department of Philosophy, Washington
University, St. Louis, MO 63130. Manuscripts should be between 35,000 and
50,000 words in length and double-spaced throughout, including quotations,
notes, and bibliography. Notes should be numbered separately for each chapter
and placed in a section at the end of the manuscript.

Richard A. Watson
Charles M. Young
—Editors

ACKNOWLEDGMENTS

MANY PEOPLE HAVE HELPED WITH THIS WORK. THEY INCLUDE A NUMBER OF graduate students, especially Susan Bradford, Louis Chenard, and Jim Thomas. Librarians play an indispensable role in such work. In this case, thanks are due particularly to the staff of the Bibliothèque Nationale in Paris, the Bibliothèque Municipale in Caen, the British Library in London, the Folger Library and the Library of Congress in Washington, the National Library of Canada, the University of Ottawa, and Carleton University in Ottawa. On four extended visits to Paris, the Fondation Nationale of the Cité Universitaire also provided hospitality at its Résidence Robert Garric. Professor Richard A. Watson and two anonymous readers made valuable suggestions and steered me away from much swampy ground. Most of all, thanks are due to Diana Armour for dozens of hours of editorial work and proofreading.

Funds for the final phase of the research and manuscript preparation were provided by the Social Sciences and Humanities Research Council of Canada.

INTRODUCTION

PASCAL'S WAGER HAS BEEN SEEN IN TERMS OF THE CALCULUS OF PROBABILI-
ties, as a piece of religious apologetic, as an event in the religious and psychological life of Pascal himself, and as an event in the life of the Jansenist movement and
its various expressions at Port-Royal. But what concerns me in this monograph is
the underlying logic of ideas brought to the surface by the intersection of two
philosophical lines of thought. Pascal, as Henri Gouhier argues, was not educated
in the tradition of Aristotelian scholasticism.[1] Indeed, he came to philosophy
largely by way of two particular strands of Platonism or neo-Platonism:[2] one,
strongly mystical, associated with the founder of the French Oratorian order,
Pierre de Bérulle; and the other, the Augustinian Platonism associated with
Duvergier de Hauranne and Cornelius Jansen. It was in these philosophical
outlooks that many of Pascal's friends at Port-Royal saw their religion,[3] and I
argue that there are strong traces of various kinds of Platonism in the *Pensées*
themselves. At the same time, Pascal was engaged in a struggle with skepticism—
as much within himself as with the Pyrrhonists to whom he refers more than
twenty times in the *Pensées* fragments.

   Pascal agrees with the skeptics that it is difficult to find God in physical nature.
His own experiments with the vacuum show that nature's abhorrence of the
vacuum, a fact commonly alleged to demonstrate that being, and so God, permeates everywhere, is simply a phenomenon of air pressure. But he disagrees with
the skeptics' claim that we know nothing of nature. The problem, indeed, is that
the human being is both "infinite" and "nothing." Our minds seem to know no
limits, and yet when we try to find ourselves as objects in nature, we find only
the mundane bodies of physics. If this reduces the force of some skeptical claims,
it surely gives rise to new ones. What if we know nothing about the world and
nothing about the knower?

   Obviously there is a problem in relating the various sorts of neo-Platonism that
influenced the Jansenists to the skepticism that Pascal thinks he must take seriously. But it may not be so obvious that each of these strands of thought was also
undergoing its own crisis. The neo-Platonism of Yves de Paris was popular in
Paris in the years just before Pascal, and it continued to be developed after him
in various forms by Nicolas de Malebranche (one of Bérulle's Oratorians) and by
the Jesuit Yves-Marie André, who was Malebranche's biographer. The traditional
neo-Platonism saw the emanations of the One everywhere and ultimately envisaged nature as returning to the One. The One, in traditional Plotinian terms, was
the source of everything and was truly without limits. Its unlimitedness was taken

so literally that the One was said to be beyond being and nonbeing. Such an unlimited source would naturally manifest itself everywhere and must ultimately, to preserve its unity, reabsorb whatever is differentiated from it. Such theories seemed not only to run into trouble with Pascal's discoveries about the vacuum but also to sit uneasily with a host of other scientific enquiries that hardly tended to show nature as reflecting the divine presence and returning, of its own power, to the One. Pascal evidently saw this neo-Platonist philosophy as headed for trouble with both science and religion.

Ideas develop over time and they are rarely intelligible if one looks at them only as they appear at a given moment; they have a future as well as a past. To understand what is going on in front of one, it is often necessary to look forward as well as backward. At the moment when Pascal wrote, the various Platonisms were showing signs of strain, and to see what worried him, it is necessary to bring the latent tensions to the surface. Fortunately, some of the philosophers who followed Pascal did that for us. As the strains grew more pressing, philosophers such as Jean-Pierre de Crousaz and Yves-Marie André (the two founders of modern philosophical aesthetics) put more and more weight on human freedom and on the need for human cooperation with the divine. In trying to reconcile their theodicies with science, they seemed increasingly to depart from what someone of Pascal's cast of mind would have thought of as Christian orthodoxy without finding anything like a scientific foundation for their beliefs.

Skepticism, too, was in a kind of crisis. The skeptic who knew what he or she was doing (who could tell doubting from believing, for instance) obviously supposed that he or she knew something about a personal state of affairs even if little or nothing could be known about the world. Descartes tried to confront this skeptic head-on. One who admits the knowledge that thinking is going on knows too much to be a good skeptic. When Pascal says Descartes is "useless,"[4] he does so not because he rejects whatever proposition is implicit in the *cogito* but because the problem is no longer that one does not know about the world but that one cannot find oneself in it. The gentlemanly skepticism of François de la Mothe le Vayer who valued the humanities and gave weight to the inner light of religion but doubted his knowledge of the external world was no longer adequate.

It is this situation—one in which we know something and yet not enough—that provokes Pascal's wager. Pascal thinks we must bet because, to be anything at all, we must rise above the nothing, and we cannot succeed through our own efforts. Human beings do have both mathematical knowledge and knowledge of their own condition as moral agents, albeit faint knowledge surrounded by darkness. The need to bet, thus, has both intellectual and moral foundations. But what are we to bet on? If we were perfectly rational, we might well bet on the God of Yves de Paris and Yves-Marie André. If we followed a good scriptural and institutional tradition, we might bet on the rule-loving God of René Rapin—the

God who has gone out of his way to make salvation easy for us. If we thought we knew *nothing at all,* we might simply resign ourselves to the nothingness. But Pascal made his bet as a man with a strong passion to believe, a certain distrust of his own rationality, and a conviction about how knowledge and doubt are to be balanced.

This is how it seems if one looks at the wager as an event in the development of Platonic and skeptical thought and allows oneself both to look for the roots of Pascal's proposals and also to look beyond Pascal to see just how some of the tensions that made him uneasy actually came to light. I do not argue that this is the only way to look at Pascal and his wager. It is only one point of view and opens only some of the possible vistas.

It does show us something about the underlying logic of the history of philosophy. If people go on looking at ideas carefully and industriously, they tend to uncover latent ideas and concepts that throw light on the whole pattern of development. Sometimes these latent features exhibit severe tensions within the ideas. Sometimes they create crises by revealing collisions with other ideas that are equally important to the world views of their holders. These developments are sometimes obscured, however, by historical developments. Some of Yves-Marie André's most interesting manuscripts, for instance, lie unpublished in the Municipal Library at Caen, not because they are worthless but because the main currents of thought and belief of his time turned away from the ideas he patiently sought to develop. Presenting Pascal's wager in this particular context also shows us something of its significance for human beings—even if it also makes us suspect that there are better bets than the one Pascal wanted us to make.

A NOTE ON THE TEXTS AND THE
NUMBERED REFERENCES TO THE *PENSÉES*

THE FIRST (ALTHOUGH INCOMPLETE) EDITION OF PASCAL'S *PENSÉES* WAS PUB-lished in Paris by Guillaume Desprez in the rue St. Jacques in June or July of 1669. It was put on sale at Port-Royal around 15 January 1670. Since then, many attempts have been made to present the fragments left by Pascal on small bits of paper in their "right order." Each attempt has produced its own numbering system.

The numbers I give for the *Pensées* in the notes are those of Louis Lafuma's Delmas editions (2 vols. Paris, 1948; rev. 1 vol. 1952, 1960), indicated as LD (I have used the one-volume edition, but the numbers are the same in all editions); those of Léon Brunschvicg (Paris: Hachette, 1950; and many earlier editions), indicated as B; and those of Lafuma's Luxembourg edition (3 vols. Paris: Editions du Luxembourg, 1951; 2d. ed. 1952; rev. 1 vol. Paris: Seuil, 1963), indicated as LL (the numbers are the same, and I have verified the entries in the one volume Seuil edition that is commonly available).

Lafuma's Delmas edition numbers are used in the generally good and easily available English translation of John Warrington in the Everyman volume, No. 874 (London: Dent, 1960) edition, which replaces the earlier Everyman Trotter translation. The Penguin edition translation by A. J. Krailsheimer uses Lafuma's Luxembourg edition numbers. It is elegant but sometimes philosophically more arguable than the Warrington translation. Lafuma's Delmas and Luxembourg numbers provide English readers with easy reference to the most available transla-tions. Many French editions and French commentators use the Brunschvicg numbers. The only other widely used order is that of Jacques Chevalier in his Gallimard Pléiade edition of Pascal's *Oeuvres complètes*, published in 1954. This is the handiest French edition of Pascal's works. It includes a table of concordance that enables the reader to move from the Brunschvicg numbers to Chevalier's numbers.

My monograph is a study of a connected set of ideas within the *Pensées* and not of the *Pensées* as a whole. What the reader needs, therefore, is an edition that brings together the ideas that belong together. The complex web of Pascal's thought has at least partially frustrated every attempt to achieve this. Lafuma's Delmas edition brings many associated ideas together, and Brunschvicg's edition brings other associations to light. Together with Chevalier's ordering, they give the reader the best chance of shedding light on and of finding the connected threads of Pascal's thought.

Louis Lafuma always defended the Delmas ordering, although scholars have lately tended to adopt the numbering of his Luxembourg edition (later published in Editions du Seuil), which generally follows the order of the Bibliothèque Nationale MS. 9203 known as *"la copie."* I am not convinced that MS. 9203 really follows Pascal's intended order even if it is, as has been argued, much more likely to be the ordering in which he left the fragments than the more traditionally used MS. 9202—*"le recueil original"*—which was obviously reorganized after his death. Lafuma also presented a case for MS. 12449, though I am not convinced by that either. The case for the Lafuma Luxembourg numbers (and so for preferring the order in MS. 9203), as well as for taking MS. 12449 seriously, is made as well as it can be by Anthony R. Pugh in *The Composition of Pascal's Apologia.*

One might be able to connect the fragments together on several levels. This *could* be done on a modern computer using directories and subdirectories, and perhaps, one day, someone will publish a "computer disk" edition of the *Pensées* organized this way. In the course of this study I made an experimental doctrinal index in an attempt to link the ideas rather than the words of the *Pensées* together. This does suggest many possible patterns, although they are too speculative for publication.

For now, it is important to remain aware of the many different orderings. In addition to the ones I have noted, the following modern editions of the *Pensées* should be borne in mind:

Zacharie Tourneur's "edition paléographique," which reproduces Bibliothèque Nationale MS. 9202, *"le recueil original,"* has detailed accounts of all the information in the manuscript.

G. Michaut's edition, published by the University of Fribourg, Switzerland, in 1896, has the ordering found in Tourneur, but without the textual apparatus.

H. F. Stewart published an ordering of his own and a translation in 1950 (London: Routledge & Kegan Paul).

Léon Brunschvicg published a facsimile edition (Paris: Hachette, 1905) of the Bibliothèque Nationale MS. 9202. There is another facsimile edition edited by Louis Lafuma (Paris: Les Librairies Associées, 1962).

There is a computerized *Concordance to Pascal's Pensées* by Hugh M. Davidson and Pierre H. Dubé (Ithaca: Cornell University Press, 1975). References to the frequencies of expressions in this monograph are taken from this indispensable work.

In the future, the standard edition of Pascal's works is likely to be the Desclée de Brouwer (Paris) edition edited by Jean Mesnard. Three volumes (1964, 1970, 1991) of the seven projected are so far available, but they do not include the *Pensées.* Volume 3 contains a serious attempt to arrange the fragments of Pascal's *Écrits sur la grace,* and I have cited it in this study.

"Infini Rien"

1

Pascal, the Wager, and the Background

1.1 A Crisis of Knowledge and a Good Bet

BLAISE PASCAL BELIEVED THAT ONE OUGHT TO WAGER ONE'S LIFE ON THE truth of the proposition that God exists; he believed, that is, that the existence of God is a good bet and that one ought to organize one's life around it and to act at all times as if God existed.[1] He believed that what one risked in such a bet is trifling and that the outcome, if one were right, would be infinitely good.

Pascal's claim is clearly, from some perspectives, outrageous. It must seem outrageous to many believers that anyone would offer betting odds not only on the existence of the deity but on God's behavior as well. It must seem outrageous to others that God would care whether or not one wagered on his existence or would be positively influenced by the fact that one did.

Philosophers are, however, as likely to be disturbed as orthodox believers. Usually, one might think, a rational bet is one based on certain sound information; for example, a horse-racing enthusiast knows that Watering Trough runs well in the mile and a quarter, prefers fast tracks, likes to pull away from a big field, and (most importantly) has been winning a lot lately. But what does Pascal know of God's track record? Does he not say, himself, that God is hidden?[2] How could one ever really know that one had won the bet? Plymouth Brethren finding themselves in the Moslem seventh heaven, filled with good things (even almond-eyed houris), might well think they had been co-opted by the devil, while devout Moslems who took the Koran literally and found themselves in the midst of solemn Plymouth Brethren, eternally singing hymns, might well think that they had been consigned to hell. What kind of knowledge does Pascal need, and can he possibly get it?

Even if Pascal could answer the epistemologist, would he not then face the skepticism of the moral philosopher and the philosopher of religion? Is there not a sense of a cleverly managed program of self-interest in Pascal's proposal? Would not many traditional elements of the supposed relation between moral theory and natural theology be hopelessly muddled if it should turn out simply

1

to be good business to believe in God? Indeed, could any being in whom it is good business to believe actually be God?

I address all of these questions in due course, but briefly, my task is, first, to put forward the argument that Pascal is best understood[3] in the context of a crisis of thought, especially in the varieties of neo-Platonism and Platonized Augustinianism of Port-Royal and elsewhere. This crisis of thought was deepened by the fact that scientific knowledge seemingly made it difficult to find not only God but also human beings in physical nature. The nature of the human being was becoming more obscure even as the nature of physical reality was becoming clearer. Thus grounds developed for a quite new kind of skepticism. The bet is a way of providing a rational response to a specific mixture of knowledge and ignorance.

Second, I argue that it was important to Pascal that his bet be a "good" one in three basic senses of *good*. A bet is "good" in the most common sense if the probability of winning and the excellence of the outcome are such that the chances of winning justify the risk. Pascal thinks this is the case about wagers on the existence of God, chiefly because he believes that the rewards to the believer will infinitely outweigh the costs and inconveniences of the bet. (We must constantly remember that one makes one's bet in this case not by putting one's money down at the two-dollar window but by *acting as if* God exists.)

But a wager would be better still if making it also increased the chances of winning. This commonly happens; for example, if a certain amount of capital is needed to create a working gold mine, then, up to the point at which the capital is attained, everyone who bets by investing in the mine helps create the desired result. In the Christian and other theistic traditions, it has always been a paradox for believers that a good God and a bad world coexist. Indeed, in the Christian tradition, God came among us, but he went unrecognized by most people and was crucified. He is, Pascal insists, hidden.[4] If we had behaved as if God existed, God would not have been crucified. If, therefore, he still exists but is in hiding, it would seem to follow that behaving as if he existed would render it more likely that he will, in fact, be manifest. That this is so follows in Pascal's mind from the fact that because the human being is God's creation, God and humanity go naturally together and have become unnaturally separated.[5] If the separation is anyone's fault, it must be ours, because God, by definition, is without fault. Therefore, correcting human faults will bring human beings closer to their natural states.[6]

Finally, any action, including any wager, will be a good one, in principle, if the goodness of the world will in fact be improved by making it and if making it does not constitute in and of itself an immoral act. Pascal thinks that behaving as if God exists will make this a better world. And behaving as if God exists is a way of behaving well, not an immoral act. He believes that this is so because one who accepts the existence of God will have to treat all people as if they were saved.[7] It is this last claim—the claim that the bet is intrinsically morally good and thus consequentially good for everyone—that I take to be most important.

1.2 Understanding Pascal in the Light of the Three Orders

My second task is to argue that this interpretation makes sense of and ultimately depends upon Pascal's doctrine that the "three orders"—essentially the intellectual order, the moral order, and the physical order[8]—are inseparably intertwined. I believe that this interconnection is central to Pascal's whole philosophy. The doctrine of the three orders provides a way of reconciling the Platonic and neo-Platonic world views with the outlook of the new sciences. Pascal believed that this reconciliation is the key to the problem. He was gripped, even more directly than Descartes, by the new sciences. Yet, far more strongly than Descartes and even more strongly than Malebranche after him, he saw the difficulties in reconciling the different sorts of truth.

His own life was punctuated occasionally by personal moral doubts (should he have dragged his feet when his sister wanted to take much of their joint patrimony with her to Port-Royal?) and animated by clear moral battles with the established order—or at any rate with that part of it whose outlook he took to be expressed by the Jesuits of his time. He saw the human condition as precarious, and he was struck even more by the fact that, despite his mathematical powers and his scientific understanding, he was very far from having a rational answer to the great questions of theology. Despite some claims to the contrary, he did not despise such rational answers. He says that God does not mean us to believe without reasons.[9] The doctrine of the three orders provides a solution that allows us to admit human frailty while framing at least a kind of answer for human doubters.

Finally, I argue that there is, given all that we know at present, a measure of plausibility to Pascal's arguments. Given certain conceptual choices, not themselves inherently unreasonable, one might well respond as Pascal did. I argue that there are real choices. If one examines closely the options open to a skeptic who challenges Pascal, one sees that Pascal has substantial reasons for thinking that for skeptics, too, a wager is in order—even if it is not quite the one envisaged.

The best reason to be interested in Pascal's wager is, surely, that once one understands what is at issue there is something to be said for it—that it helps us to see the options that a reasonable human being ought to consider. But another reason is that there remains a natural interest in an issue about which much ink has been spilt without anyone's having come up with an account that seems quite worthy of a man of Pascal's intellect and sensitivity. Pascal lived only thirty-nine years (from 1623 to 1662), in the course of which he created a good part of probability theory, invented and built a digital calculator, made important advances in differential calculus, created the first Paris bus service, and fought a long-running battle with the Jesuit order, which sometimes forced him into hiding. His friends, who included the men and women who made Port-Royal, for a few years, the storm center of French intellectual and religious life, were desolated at his death. Some of them, at least, evidently believed the fragments of *Pensées* he left held, if they could but be put in their right order,[10] the prospect of a serious Christian apologetic.

It must be admitted that overall, whether he was investigating the theory of the vacuum or exploring the moral codes he took to be recommended by the Jesuits, he never seemed to be foolish. He could be unfair—he often was to the Jesuits—but he almost always seems to combine a gift for logical analysis with strong moral conviction. He could also be obsessive, as the same documents suggest. Furthermore, he seemed to feel himself burdened by some great weight— a weight strangely attached to all human beings even though, he said, a human being is only a "thinking reed." The obsessions and the sense of burden—the word *fear* (*peur*) occurs sixteen times in the *Pensées*—may make us wonder whether Pascal's mind was not precariously balanced, but those who face up to the apparent realities of the world must often know the meaning of these emotions.

The investigation seems worth continuing, therefore, until we are convinced that we understand the wager.

1.3 Pascal and Self-Interest

In the recent tradition of English-speaking analytic philosophy, it has been most common to see the wager as one tied to the calculation of self-interest. And this does seem to be what one finds on the surface of the fragment. In these terms, some writers have derived two or even three different arguments from Pascal's formulation. Ian Hacking finds three: one is simply that if God exists, he will save the believers and damn the unbelievers. This argument depends on the dominance of God if he exists at all. We may not know for certain that the existence of God is even possible, yet if, as Pascal thinks, the cost to the believer is not too great, belief is reasonable. This argument does not depend on any particular view about the probability of the existence of God. The second argument is that the existence and nonexistence of God are equiprobable and that, therefore, belief is clearly the best bet if, in fact, there are only two options. The third argument Hacking postulates is that the existence of God is at least possible, and therefore it has some finite probability. This version gives, perhaps, less ground for belief than the second but somewhat more than the first.[11]

Peter C. Dalton argues in somewhat the same vein in two articles.[12] He, too, claims that in Pascal's text there is one argument that contains no specific claim about the probability that God exists and one in which the probability is one-half. Hacking thinks that Pascal has hold of something useful, but that the difficulty is that the alternatives are not exhaustive. There might be many different sorts of possible beings and many different sorts of theological policies to bet on. Dalton also argues that the probability that God exists cannot be known to be one-half, but he claims that the argument that does not depend on specific probabilities is unsound, because Christianity, on Pascal's account, ought to be judged so unfathomable that the believer does not know what he is betting on.

I shall raise questions about rationality, practical reason, probability, and the kind of knowledge that we might have of the existence of God and of the structure of Christianity. But I doubt that these formulations, in any case, capture much of what interested Pascal. The self-interest of the believer is put forward as being the believer's own interest in being personally saved or damned, and the argument is made out to be one to the effect that God is more likely to save those who believe than to save those who refuse to believe. God, that is, is thought to be disturbed by the lack of belief and to be generally vengeful.

Indeed, P. T. Landsberg specifically claims that the whole argument depends on the belief in God's vengefulness,[13] and certainly the self-interest in believing a version of the argument would seem to lead in that direction. But if so, the argument could be disposed of very quickly. Terence Penelhum argues cogently that the vengeance policy ascribed to God is surely immoral.[14] If so, then belief in God furthers this immorality and would amount, itself, to an immoral activity.

Nicholas Rescher in an extended study notices that the underlying issues have to do with hope and trust and that the question to be assessed is the effect, overall, of that hope and trust on the whole situation; but he also paints the question, generally, as one of rational self-interest. The essence of the matter, says Rescher, is given in "one assumption kept constant throughout—the view of the human being as prudently self-preoccupied, proceeding with a calculating view to rational self-interest."[15] He admits, in the same passage, that "this is doubtless not the noblest and most elevated sort of religious faith."

It is important, however, not to misunderstand Rescher. It does not follow from this that moral and properly religious considerations have no place in the "calculations."[16] Suppose that one values morality above all else. Rescher's account simply suggests that one would be prudent to act in such a way, in that case, as to make morality as likely as possible. Again, if one thinks that the furtherance of religious practice and belief is most important, one will try to act so as to make religious practice and belief as likely as possible. What is at issue is one's reason (or reasons) for doing these things.

Immanuel Kant also supposed that practical reason must be employed to prove the existence of God, but he believed that it would be immoral to argue in the way that Rescher ascribes to Pascal. Morality requires not just that one act morally but that one act morally because it is good or right to act morally and not because there is some advantage in it. Kant's version of the "practical argument" has no undisputed reading either, but a plausible version that helps to make the point here goes as follows: The existence of God is a necessary postulate of pure practical reason, essentially because the existence of duty implies the *summum bonum* in its guise as the *bonum consummatum* (the good as an actual perfection). This, in turn, requires the reconciliation of happiness (a species of self-interest on the usual views) and duty, because one's right to happiness is, on the face of it, as fundamental as one's commitment to duty. Indeed, it is because these two are sometimes in apparent conflict that the problem of morality arises in a serious way. If that reconciliation of self-interest (or happiness) and duty could not be guaranteed, we would have a duty to bring about what we cannot bring about, namely the *summum bonum*. And to have a duty to do what one cannot involves a contradiction or at least a meaningless proposal. What is one to do? What one is furthering in seeking the resolution is not self-interest but the *summum bonum* as the *bonum consummatum*.[17]

Rescher's reply to Kant is that Pascal's version of the bet is not immoral because it is not *worldly* self-interest that is at issue.[18] Rather, what is involved is a kind of eternal and universal interest, which, partly because it is associated with God and God's will, is no longer "crass." It is immune, thus, to the Kantian objection that one should not pursue self-interest for its own sake. What is being pursued is part of what is needed for the *bonum consummatum*.

Rescher also has answers to many of the claims that this kind of argument, even if it were Pascal's, would simply be invalid. It has often been claimed that Pascal has not defined the alternatives clearly, that he has not taken account of various non-Christian beliefs, and that he certainly, therefore, does not give his reader an exhaustive set of options. It is even true, Rescher says, that one in the state of mind produced by Pascal's argument would not seem very worthy of salvation. But a *practical* argument is always aimed at giving someone in some particular situation a reason for doing something or other. Hence, he says, the fact that Pascal does not consider various rival polytheistic views and so forth is not an issue.[19] Rescher thinks that the persons to whom the argument is directed must be "those nominal Christians, whose name is legion, who do indeed espouse the god-conception on which the argument is premised."[20] As for the claim that believers in Pascal's argument would be unfit for salvation, Rescher answers that betting on God's existence does not guarantee salvation, but it opens the way to a further development.

Rescher is not very interested in the historical questions about what Pascal really meant. He begins by saying that his is "emphatically not an exercise in Pascal scholarship or exegesis." [21] But he does attack Jules Lachelier for being ahistorical in overstating Pascal's use of the idea that one must renounce self-interest.[22] Lachelier argues that Pascal equates salvation with renouncing self-interest and renunciation of self-interest with admission of the existence of God. Rescher says that this argument "just is not Pascal's."[23]

The problem with Rescher's account, however, is that his reading does not bring out the issues that are philosophically most interesting and does not place Pascal in his own context. In Rescher's view, the argument is addressed only to people in a certain frame of mind. But these "nominal Christians" of whom Rescher speaks, although of interest to historians and sociologists of religion, are of no special philosophical interest.

We must ask, anyhow, what *Pascal* actually would have to say about readings such as Rescher's. In so far as Rescher's argument is based on the notion that a real self-interest properly belongs to those in certain states of mind that would be advanced by belief, Pascal's verdict would be scathing and would force one to give up any such reading as being his own. Pascal insists that self-love is the beginning of all disorder and also that it is contrary to justice.[24] It is the essence of concupiscence (understood as the strong desire for worldly things and not, as is sometimes the case, merely as sexual desire), and it belongs to the *second* human nature, which emerges only after the Fall.

There is not a *real* self-interest, for this "self" is, after all, literally nothing. As much as Cardinal Bérulle, Pascal believed that the human being, as such, is nothing[25] and that we become something only in relation to God. Rescher, certainly, concedes that self-interest must, based on Pascal's view, be transformed into some divine interest. But the wager must link the present human being with humanity as it ought to be. It is human beings here and now who make the wager. And it is not in their interest (as corrupt beings) to do so. The wager must, however, motivate them, not the transformed beings, and therefore the argument must be conceived, I believe, in some other way.

It is easy enough to understand how Rescher's interpretation gets started, because bets are normally made by rational beings in their own self-interest. And there has to be some element of *ordinary* betting involved, first, because Pascal himself was no doubt a betting man and, second, because he would not have wanted to mislead his readers by using language that set them on a wrong course. The Rescher argument, if it cannot be wholly right, cannot be altogether wrong, either.

A solution to this difficulty—and to much else—is in Pascal's account of the three orders.[26] There is an order of the body, the physical realm; an order of the mind, the intellectual realm; and an order of charity, the moral realm. Rational arguments may appeal to the situation in any order, but a genuine philosophical argument ought to appeal to the just proportion between them. The difficulty is to find this just proportion. Arguments that appeal to our bodily states may, for instance, be legitimate arguments based on our need to respond to hunger or fatigue. Arguments that appeal to our minds or intellects may well, of course, appeal to our rational, intellectual self-interest. The wager, in the first instance, obviously does both, but it is meant to lead us to see that we need to appeal to our charitable instincts—to something that comes, Pascal thinks, from the supernatural.

How might this be so? The wager, in fact, forces one to the central question: What should I do with my life? In terms of the three orders, there would seem to be different answers. I can commit myself to some attempt to achieve the well-being of my body. By sticking strictly to the terms of one's awareness of one's body, one commits oneself to a life of pleasure and of avoidance of pain. In what are now common philosophical terms, this is the answer of the hedonistic utilitarian. In seventeenth-century language (which sounds more pejorative), this was often imagined to be the life of the libertine, a name usually assigned to skeptics but that had overtones suggesting one who believed whatever he or she wanted to believe. A carefully controlled version of such a life, the life of the Stoic, was certainly one of the options known to Pascal and his friends.

Second, I can devote my life to the well-being of the mind. That is to say, I can do what reason commends when reason is harnessed to the attempts of the intellect to consider my well being, for at this point it is still, literally, "my" well being.

Third, I can appeal to the order of charity. When Pascal uses the famous phrase "the heart has its reasons,"[27] he is talking about the order of charity. This order is primarily the moral realm, although it may well, also, be the set of reasons based on "insight" that gives one a clue about reality.[28] Basically, though, the French *charité*, from the Latin *caritas*, has to do with caring, and caring for others is Pascal's notion of morality. One who does this is, as we sometimes say, one who has a heart. Once we have seen how the wager forces the question of morality on us, we can see, easily enough, how the wager argument goes and why Pascal talks about the choice between infinity and nothing. The body, taken by itself, is doomed (i.e., without reference to the possibility that God may exist and may resurrect it, it has no hope at all). Bodily pleasures are momentary and we all die. Thus the body's only hope is in a resurrection. In anticipating Matthew Arnold (himself a close student of seventeenth-century thought), this becomes, in any case, a moral matter. The resurrection is about the claim that goodness, itself, cannot be destroyed.[29] If we are to be resurrected, Pascal would say, it can be only because goodness demands it. And this takes us beyond the moral order. And what of the life of the intellect? The reasons of the heart, he says, are unknown to the intellect. But that is because the intellect, in this sense, is committed to its function as *my* intellect. In any case, "reason can be made to serve any purpose."[30]

Reason cannot make the necessary decisions, because it sets up antinomies and contradictions if it is understood as something that *provides* the moral truth. But if it is understood as pointing beyond itself, as showing us that we need an objective goal in life that cannot be supplied simply by reason, then it can be seen as having a moral dimension. But to what does it point? Presumably, it points to what is not limited in the way that reason is. But everything in this world is limited either because it is a defined physical entity or because it cannot be an end in itself. Because the argument leads beyond itself, there is clearly a difficulty. It is not now *my life* in the original sense that is at issue, for we have passed that. It is, as it were, my life seen as a facet of the infinite. Self-interest is therefore in some measure bypassed. The obvious difficulty if one presses the matter this far is that we cannot now really talk, as Rescher does, in terms of rational self-interest at all. But the argument proceeds by an appeal to self-interest that then bypasses self-interest. Does it then destroy itself?

If one still has any doubts, consider that the whole thrust of the *Lettres Provinciales,*[31] mostly devoted to Pascal's attack on the Jesuit Order, was against this kind of religion of calculated self-interest. But we are not yet quite through with this line of interpretation.

1.4 *Contre les libertins?*

It has been suggested, of course, that the wager is intended only for libertines, essentially for those who are already skeptics who feel free to disbelieve what they please. Such an argument is appropriate for them, especially if being free to disbelieve what one pleases implies the freedom to believe what one pleases. (If there are *no* constraints on belief, or if one can really disbelieve freely, one should be able to believe freely as well.) Such suggestions come from philosophers as eminent as Léon Brunschvicg and Jacques Chevalier.[32] Chevalier emphasizes the moral overtones of the term *libertine*. He associates skeptics with *joueurs,* gamblers. The views of libertines were not originally based on self-interest but on the notion—the *fact* they might rather have said—that nothing ultimately *compels* one to most of the beliefs that philosophers and ordinary citizens have taken to be necessary.

In these circumstances, the wager might be taken to urge restoration of the belief in the existence of God on the ground that even one who is wholly able to believe anything that he or she pleases would find that the rewards for a winning bet still infinitely outweigh the displeasure that may result from carrying out the believing program. There are obvious objections to this reading, not least that what Pascal had in mind was not simply intellectual belief (whatever that might be) but a passionate commitment to treat others as if they were saved. Still, the libertines, or at least the Pyrrhonists, as he in fact preferred to call them, played an important role in Pascal's thinking and have almost the last word in this monograph.[33] It would be hard, indeed, to overestimate their role.[34]

Pascal begins one fragment with the words "Pyrrhonism is true."[35] This quotation, which Terence Penelhum places at the head of a chapter on Pascal, led him to conclude that Pascal was a skeptical fideist.[36] But in another place, Pascal says that "nature confounds the Pyrrhonist."[37] The claim that Pyrrhonism is true is merely the assertion that, before Jesus, philosophers got their religion wrong; and the claim that Pyrrhonism is confounded has to do both with our tendency to believe and with the availability of scientific accounts of nature. Yet Pascal says, in the same passage, that the "dogmatist" is confounded by reason, which always presents us with alternatives. Pascal believes, that is, that we know enough to bet and not enough to be sure, and so, as he claims, what he proposes is to provide a religious apologetic addressed to the human condition, and there is probably, as Per Lønning argues,[38] good reason to believe him.

Henri Gouhier considers the possibility that the "mathematical libertine" is being addressed by the wager, but he is cautious. He suggests that the wager is a link between the parts of the *Pensées* that address the human condition and the parts that address the need for religious belief.[39]

Although the "message for the libertines" doctrine *is* advanced by both Brunschvicg and Chevalier, neither is able to believe that Pascal was as crass as the self-interest argument seems to suppose. One way of reconciling these views would be to hold that the argument is simply directed to the spurious or apparent self of the libertine and that its soundness (though not, of course, its formal validity) is, indeed, destroyed as soon as all possible premises about the reality and importance of self-interest are seen to be false. The libertine, after all, does have a problem. A freethinker is committed to no ultimate metaphysical beliefs about the self and yet claims either to be able to doubt (i.e., to indulge in a rational mental activity that extends over time) or to be able to withhold beliefs (a practice that requires enough knowledge to be able to tell when one is believing or not). There is a sense, therefore, in which the libertine, or any skeptic, makes do with a kind of illusion of the continuing self accepted for purposes of argument without any ultimate commitment.

But Pascal does not approach the libertine or the skeptic (if there is a difference between them) directly with an argument designed to show that their beliefs about themselves and their selfhood are either false or susceptible of logical confusion. In fact, Pascal must be sympathetic to those caught in conflicts of doubt and belief, for he thinks we must realize that the human being *is*—really is—both "infinite and nothing," the expression with which Pascal begins the wager fragment. Many of the standard ways of attacking the skeptic are simply not open to Pascal, and we must suppose that he was constantly aware of this fact.

Thus, he does not say anything at all that suggests that his argument is intended to be less than universal. On the contrary, it is not his view that one simply bypasses one's "baser" or illusory self and becomes a being fit for a pure, Platonic order of charity. Pascal holds, rather, that one always has a bodily and a mental nature whether one is a libertine or not and that the order of charity is possible only for those who find a right proportion among the three orders.

The intellect enters the realm of charity only by recognizing its own limitations: "The greatness of man is great in that he recognizes himself as pitiable."[40] Unless the intellect sees itself in proportion to the order of charity, it fails. But it is capable of seeing this, although, within the order of the intellect, there is no mention of charity. Charity does not rate a description in physics texts. It is not that the physical human being is unimportant—medicine may have much to say about human nature—it is just that neither physics nor its applications have anything to say about the intellect proper nor anything to say about the good.

One can, as Pascal noticed, have a quite perfect body and an intellect that produces nothing, and one can have an intellect that is unsurpassed without having—or needing—"worldly or intellectual eminence." No one can explain why the order of charity does not equally embrace everyone.

Nevertheless, religious men and women and human beings whose affairs are directed by the order of charity—Ignatius, Mother Theresa, or Mère Angélique at Port-Royal—turn out to have *practical* concerns and skills as well as the other kinds. But the source of this practical charity is in another philosophical insight, not in the Cartesian intellectual philosophy that Pascal held to be "useless, uncertain, and troublesome."[41] This other kind of philosophy is, evidently, the one that Pascal hopes to put forward in the *Pensées*. To investigate further, we must turn to the historical context.

2

The Platonic Elements
in the Historical Context

2.1 The Idea of Infinity and Pascal's Natural Theology

BLAISE PASCAL SURELY CANNOT HAVE BEEN A FIDEIST WHO SUPPOSED THAT though we know nothing, we ought to believe much. One does not bet on something about which one knows *nothing*.

Readers, however, have often drawn upon the words Pascal uses in the wager fragment: "We are therefore incapable of knowing what he [God] is or whether he is."[1] They take this as suggesting that Pascal believed that he knew nothing— rendering his wager nugatory at the outset. But they forget that, to begin with, he had already said in the same fragment, "We know that the infinite exists without knowing its nature." The support for this claim to knowledge, in so far as one is given in the same fragment, is this: We know at least one objective truth about it; namely, that infinity plus or minus one remains the same quantity. This is obvious to Pascal and to anyone else, I suppose, who retains a doctrine like that of the three orders. To exist is to have a place in one or more such orders. One of the orders is the intellectual order; infinity clearly exists there. Whether it exists anywhere else is another matter.

The infinite, the unlimited, is the most common metaphysical subject matter of seventeenth-century natural theology. The only other property of God that attracted so much attention is his indivisibility, and generally, infinity and indivisibility went hand in hand. The absolute cause (or substance) of Eustachius a Sancto Paulo (a thinker admired and probably drawn upon by Descartes); the one, ultimate, final, or real substance of Descartes; the neo-Platonic supreme unity of Yves de Paris and Cardinal Bérulle; the God of Spinoza; and the infinite idea that figures (not much later) in the works of Malebranche are all species of this infinity.

Pascal gave infinity his own twist by exploring some of its mathematical properties, especially the fact that infinity plus one and infinity minus one are the same number as infinity itself. This is evidently of great importance to him in his conflict with the skeptics, "*les pyrrhoniens*," as he nearly always calls them. His conclusion is that, while nature confounds the skeptics,[2] reason confounds the dogmatists. Our natures lure us into belief, of course, but "nature" reveals a certain order in things even if there is some doubt about applying pure reason (in its form as mathematics) to nature.[3] Even so, there is hope. Mathematics preserves the order of things[4] even if nature has often proved very puzzling.[5]

This is intelligible if we notice that Pascal seems to be assuming that the skeptic is committed to some elementary mathematics. No fragment spells out this commitment in detail, but we may suppose that the skeptic must be able to count. If one is simply withholding belief, one must know that the number of one's beliefs is zero. If one supposes that one can actively doubt *all* propositions (or any proposition whatsoever), one needs to believe something more surprising, for the number of such propositions is infinite, and to know that one can doubt infinitely many propositions is to know a great deal.

If one does not admit that one can count reliably, one cannot know that the number of one's beliefs is zero, and if one does not admit the concept of infinity, one must hold that the number of propositions one can doubt is finite. More of the context of these questions is given in the next chapter (in the discussion of the three orders), and in the last chapter I address them in detail.

In posing the questions, Pascal has in mind people such as François de la Mothe le Vayer. La Mothe le Vayer—sometimes at least—combined skepticism about science with a fideistic belief in a religion that need meet no tests of reason.[6] Pascal says that people who hold very extravagant opinions fuel Pyrrhonism in two ways.[7] One is obvious: If believers assert ridiculous propositions, their hearers become skeptical of almost everything. The other is a little less obvious but can be seen in the work of people such as La Mothe le Vayer. Here skepticism is a two-edged sword. The more one finds that there is no special reason to believe in any particular well-attested truth (such as the claims of science), the more one is free to believe what one chooses, for one logical outcome of a complete propositional skepticism is that all propositions are equally doubtful. If so, one can believe one as well as another. One does not have to give reasons for one's beliefs if no good reasons can be given for *any* propositions.

It is thus very important to Pascal that skeptics should have to accept some arithmetic. But his concerns about infinity are real. One can (and must) admit that the infinite exists;[8] but if there is a real infinite in the sense intended, does it not transcend everything that we know? Is it not so unlike us as to have, as he suggests, "no relation" to us?[9] That the infinite number does not change if we add one to it or deduct one from it is something we all now agree about. If God is infinite in this sense, how could what we do make any difference to him? It might be, of course, that this property of being able to delete quantities while remaining the same would allow God to shed many properties (in the process of becoming a man, for instance) while yet remaining the same, but if these experiences add nothing to his nature, how does he know what he has done? Second, suppose we could say something or other about the infinite. What has it to do with the God who is supposed to save us?

The answer Pascal would give is *not* "nothing at all." The wager fragment contains, near the beginning, the words "God's justice must be as vast as his mercy."[10] That is, *if* God exists in more than the intellectual realm and is associated with the infinite, he must have the qualities of the infinite. Whatever qualities he has will, presumably, be infinite, and whatever he wants to achieve, he will be able to achieve to an infinite extent. If he is merciful, his mercy will be infinite, and if he is concerned with justice, his justice will be infinite.

We do not know for certain that God has these qualities. But we do know that we are to choose between the infinite and nothing. Thus, the first words of the wager fragment are the enigmatic "Infinity nothing"—words that appear in the text with no punctuation between them.[11]

Pascal takes up one of the preoccupations of the natural theologians of his time; concerns about infinity are for him central. This is reason enough to enquire into how some of the natural theologies of the time actually worked. There is another reason as well. Pascal evidently thought that the more we discover about the infinite being as a kind of polar concept in our metaphysical constructions, the more difficult it may be to associate such a being with the God with whom he is concerned—the God of morality who is involved in salvation.

For him to save us, God must involve himself in the finitude of our affairs. He must, indeed, in so doing, disguise himself as a finite agent. If we take him simply as an infinite being, nothing about him changes with the addition or subtraction of any finite quantity. Supposing God did want to save us, how, if he became human, could even he recognize himself? (In two of the Gospels, the last words of Jesus are "My God, my God, why hast thou forsaken me?"[12])

Somehow, the gap must be bridged, and Pascal believes that it can be. If one doubts that he was himself a kind of neo-Platonist, one need only look at his letter to his sister Mme Périer (signed jointly with his other sister, Jacqueline), written on 1 April 1648. There he specifically invokes Plato's image of the cave and speaks of the whole universe as a place in which the visible world is a device used by God to represent the invisible by the visible.[13]

Furthermore, contrary to those who seem to believe that Pascal thought the relation of God to the world totally mysterious, he writes (in what is surely an accompanying fragment to the wager fragment) about how we can *conceptualize that relation precisely*. Consider, he says, "a point moving everywhere at an infinite speed."[14] There we have something "infinite and indivisible"—the two properties most talked about in God. I do not know whether Pascal thought that such a thing existed literally or existed only as a very important possibility.

Suppose there were such a particle. If it traveled infinitely fast it would be, as he says again, "everywhere."[15]

What bothered Pascal was the question about how God, *even* so conceived, could interfere in our world. If he genuinely shared whatever kind of being we have, would he not be indistinguishable from us? It is not so much a question of whether or not God could do this. He has infinite energy at his disposal, and he is already everywhere. It is a question about how we make contact with him.

What if he did not appear to us at all? Then I think it was Pascal's view that he would not really exist as God. As a being whose locus excluded the physical world—who existed in the intellectual and perhaps (in some sense) in the moral order—he could well be the creature of the philosophers, a legitimate concern of the intellect. But to be genuinely the god relevant to humanity, he must not only span all the orders but appear to us as well.

If one supposes that there is, in reality, a problem about how God, in whatever way he is conceivable in the physical world, can actually interfere in our affairs, the bet Pascal proposes arises just because our actual—and even potential—information about God stops short of the point at which it would become decisive for our lives.

2.2 The Infinite and the Indivisible in the Thought of Pascal's Era

To explain what is at issue, I shall examine the ideas of the infinite and the indivisible as they occurred to some people who thought about them at the time that Pascal was writing. The relevant cast of characters includes some philosophers who are now fairly obscure—Eustachius a Sancto Paulo and Yves de Paris—and Pierre de Bérulle, whose name and whose main deeds as founder of the French Oratorian Order[16] are better known than his ideas. It also includes, of course, Descartes, who was nearly always at stage center as the philosophical dramas of this period unfolded.

I begin with Bérulle whose mixture of rationalism and mysticism parallels Pascal's own. Pierre de Bérulle was strongly influenced by the fifteenth-century Italian thinker, Nicholas of Cusa, a man for whom the unity of God, the ultimate unity of humanity and God and of nature and God, took precedence over everything and for whom knowledge of everything other than God was knowledge of negations through which God himself was to be known. The Oratorians were generally freethinkers, and the mavericks of Catholic thought—from Malebranche to John Henry Newman—have always been attracted to them. They took only temporary vows. In France, they had a central organization (under Bérulle), although in Italy they did not even have that.

Bérulle was a mystic in religion, but he was also attracted to science.[17] He praised Copernicus.[18] He was, in short, a rational mystic in a tradition that has its origins in Augustine and which includes the Pseudo-Dionysius, Nicholas of Cusa, and Meister Eckhart. Much of the Pascalian notion of the "hidden God" and the idea that the human being is nothing in itself are found in Bérulle's *Grandeurs de Jésus*. But Bérulle could allow that the intellect could take us back to an understanding of our ultimate inseparability from God, while Pascal is uneasy about how we can cross such an infinite distance.

Pascal begins his fragment with the words *"infini rien,"*[19] and the sentiment is one that can readily be found in Bérulle as well. In *Opuscules* 10 and 13 of his *Opuscules de piété*,[20] he insists that humanity is nothing, is created from nothing, and has its being only in God. Indeed, he praises Copernicus in part because Copernicus sees that our world is not the center of the universe and that it derives its being from another source.

Bérulle has a way out of Pascal's difficulty about the human inability to cross the infinite gulf that separates us from God. God manifests himself through three emanations: Nature, Grace, and the *"Union hypothétique."*[21] God appears in and through nature itself but distinguishes himself from it first through the idea of grace and then, finally, by joining in it through the Incarnation.

There is thus a measure of reality to each element in the triad even though all depend, finally, on God and are unintelligible without him. We can set ourselves apart from nature through an act of divine grace, and we can establish our genuine independence through the license given to human beings in the Incarnation. From being nothing, we become partners—but we lapse into nothingness again if we give up the partnership, for then we are merely natural objects.

Our animal nature thus can be overcome. The situation is full of perils both conceptual and practical. Yet Bérulle is optimistic.

He is employing here a mixture of philosophical and scriptural arguments together with an element of mystical experience. Philosophically, he argues that everything is an ultimate unity and only God is, finally, real—for there is nothing left over from the nature of God out of which a world can be made. Yet we know from our scientific knowledge that there is a natural world with laws of its own—a world that can be and is studied to great effect.

One must ask: How can this be? Nothingness cannot have laws of its own. One answer was given by Yves de Paris: God, too, is bound by certain laws of logic, especially the law of contrariety. But Bérulle is disinclined to associate the ultimate unity of God with any principle of diversity, and indeed, he is disinclined to think that natural knowledge is enough to solve the problem. Nature must be, indeed, on logical grounds, an emanation of God, but we must draw upon revelation for the rest of the answer. Scripture assures us that God has implanted his grace in the world—that is, he has ordered it so it is not merely naturally good but so it can reflect his own nature as well. This grace shows itself in human reason and human knowledge. Yet that very possibility entails the possibility of error, for human knowledge is a reflection of the natural world through our own natures. This establishes a new viewpoint in the universe, the human viewpoint, and each human being can therefore choose to turn his knowledge to his or her own ends. This is how sin becomes possible and, indeed, actual. The return to God from this state is possible only through a further divine intervention in the form of the Incarnation. But the Incarnation involves humanity in an act of belief. Thus, in his *Grandeurs de Jésus,* Bérulle insists that God comes to earth "hidden as a man."[22]

This situation poses Pascal's problem. Based on Bérulle's account, we can understand the world through an act of faith. It all makes sense if we undertake that act of faith, but natural knowledge is not enough. It does not occur to Bérulle that this is a gamble in Pascal's sense, but this is because the final gap in his thought is filled by direct experience. If we experience our oneness with God and if that experience when combined with philosophical argument and scriptural analysis ultimately makes sense, then we are justified. The final judgment is associated with what Newman much later called the "illative sense," the moment of insight in which one sees that the whole picture fits together. Pascal, however, seems—perhaps because of his own very different kind of mystical experience[23]— suspicious of this last element. It would, in any case, give a kind of certainty to what, for him, can never be certain.

But in very many ways, Pascal's devout but unorthodox outlook, with its mixture of science and scripture, is closer to that of Bérulle than to almost any other thinker of the time, because like Pascal, Bérulle is trying to find a clear place for humanity between the infinite and the nothingness. Later, Malebranche and Yves-Marie André struggle with this task, but it involves finding something in the natural world that natural science does not find there—real traces of the hidden God. The more one presses it, the more one confronts the scientific account of the world. Equally, the more one establishes a role for humanity between the infinite and the nothingness, the more one adds to the stature of humanity, lessening human dependence on God. Bérulle wants to avoid religious scandal by making humanity's being a mere reflection of God's. But this creates a tension in his system; the less reality he gives to the human being, the less the human person is able to reach out to God and the less, perhaps, each of us is able to assess our own experiences, even our mystical ones.

Yves de Paris, a Capuchin monk, was among the most popular of the apologists of the period.[24] His *Digestum Sapientiae,* an eleven hundred-page summary of all knowledge organized on a neo-Platonic pattern derived from Raymond Lull (1235–1315), was much admired. Yves adapted not only the philosophy of Lull but also that of Nicholas of Cusa. He believed that reality is an ultimate and indivisible unity and that God produces the world according to what Yves calls the law of contraries—that is, God, in order to create a world out of unity must create things that exclude one another. This creates the false illusion of a world composed of individual bits and pieces of things, but reality is really united, as Plato had thought, by the form of the good.

The problem for our enquiry is that such views, common enough in Paris at the time, pose a problem about how the moral order is related to the other orders. How can we understand how the good becomes fragmented, and how can we rise above the disunity to the unity?

Yves believed that all appearances are misleading, but by means of a form of the "negative theology," we can arrive at a measure of the truth sufficient for our needs. He did deliberate battle with the Port-Royalists, especially Antoine Arnauld,[25] but Pascal does not actually mention Yves by name.[26] He cannot, however, have failed to hear of him, and no doubt his objection to this kind of natural theology must be that, on such a view, the abstract unity absorbs everything, and the significance of our individual actions becomes obscure. It would seem that we need only understand the whole and that we need not do anything, but this seems to run counter to morality.

Yves belonged to the tradition according to which reality is ultimately a unity. In this unity, knowledge results from discerning in the flux of what is presented the ideas that shape being by informing the particulars that compose the perceptible world. This view has theological advantages. If it is true, God and the world intersect in such a way that God might not be as difficult to find as the Cartesians seem to make him. And he might not necessarily be involved in every morsel of knowledge. It is even fairly easy to understand such a world picture in terms of Newtonian physics. Isaac Newton was influenced by the Cambridge Platonists who exhibited *some* of the strands of thought found in Yves de Paris.[27]

The advantages of Yves' view as well as its relation to the Newtonian view can be seen by contrasting it with the Aristotelian view of scientific knowledge. The Aristotelian view is that knowledge (or more exactly the intelligibility of the world) is gained by examining individual things, events, or states of affairs. From these individuals, the mind or intellect abstracts general properties, which it orders according to principles of explanation. In the Aristotelian systems, these principles of explanation are generally related to the essences of things, and from the essences of things their overall tendencies or final causes can be inferred. But this part of the story is not necessary; neither essentialism nor the theory of final causes needs to be associated with the Aristotelian view of knowledge as abstraction from matter, and the seventeenth-century reformers quickly dropped these notions in favor of accounts of general laws. These general laws, however, are to be understood as being supported by the specific instances on which they are based. David Hume undercut this kind of inductivism in the next century.

The Newtonian view is that there are certain standard patterns natural to the universe and that deviations from them are to be explained. One of Newton's laws of motion is that bodies continue in a uniform direction at a uniform velocity unless they are interfered with. No one has ever discovered an instance of this uniform motion, so what has to be explained are the deviations from the general law. In fact, bodies do not attract one another directly as their mass and indirectly as the square of the distance between them because, inevitably, there are other forces at work; the deviations from this great "inverse square rule" are to be explained.

Actual things, in fact, are instances of general ideas—imperfect instances because the variety of things in the world influences each and every item, forcing them all to adapt, and thus driving each away from the perfection of the archetypes. This is the view of Yves de Paris. Newtonian science goes on to explain these deviations.

If everything is derived from a fundamental pattern, then this pattern must exhibit some kind of unity. But if everything we actually find also exhibits particularity and so a measure of deviation from principle, then there must be an explanation for this deviation.

Yves' most basic principles are these:

1. The fundamental ordering force in the universe is the idea of the good. This idea is identical to the idea of the infinite and complete unity. The heart and essence of the idea of God is the idea of the good. Thus God acts in orderly ways and always in accordance with the good.

2. The world is formed from the idea of the good—which contains all the elements that go to make up whatever is best—by the principle of contrariety. This principle demands that if anything is a particular instance of a principle, it must be accompanied by a complementary entity that limits its being.

3. Nothing in the universe is ultimately separable from anything else in an absolute way; nothing can change unless everything changes. This holds good for knowledge itself and for the relation between the knower and the known.

The main line of argument in defence of these principles is this: Our experience of the world is, certainly, of a universe of discrete entities. Yet we see, in fact, that they all form a single system. The world of science is one in which explanations take the form of universal laws, and no one of these laws is intelligible in isolation. Our experience also forms a unity; we can distinguish elements within it, but we do not find elements that are absolutely independent.

The central fact about the world, then, is that it is a unity that expresses itself in an apparent diversity. The only way in which we can understand absolute unity is by appeal to the intellect. The *"raisons sensibles"* promised in the subtitle to Yves' *Théologie naturelle* are the testimony of experience that shows that reality is a unity but does not tell what that unity is like. So we must turn to *"les raisons moralles,"* that is, to the workings of the intellect.[28]

This unity is only "intelligible" on condition that we can understand a kind of unity that would have to be expressed through a necessary diversity. Thus in his *Théologie naturelle*, Yves brings forth the law of contrariety that he uses so extensively.[29] His explanation is that if the unity were to manifest itself in a particular way in any possible world, it would have to manifest itself as something or other. But to be something or other is always to exclude being something else. A patch of paint cannot be red if it does not exclude being green. Nothing can be tall without failing to be short. But the unity without limit—the unity in itself—could not fail to have the capacity for all the contraries. Therefore it is only approximately expressed in the world.

We can, perhaps, get a little closer to the nature of this unity because we know that evil is always a lack, and therefore that the One—which lacks nothing—is good. This is its claim to be God. It therefore must order all things, as far as this is possible, for the best, but allow for the fact that every particular world excludes something that would be good and orders things in such a way as to create imperfections. Admittedly, we ourselves are among the imperfections of the world. We are finite creatures. Yet we are intimately related to the whole, not as any part of the whole but because our experience itself reflects this unity, and our knowledge enables us to reproduce it in our intellectual work.

In one sense it is not so astonishing that it is through humanity that God comes into the world, for the human being is by nature a particular capable of representing the whole. That this capability should not be merely potential but should come to reality is, of course, given the possibilities for evil and our own corrupt natures, a miracle. But miracles, too, must make sense. Unintelligible events cannot be miracles. Indeed, it is only because there is a sound foundation of intelligibility in natural theology that revelation is intelligible to us.

Yves, to be sure, rather exalts humanity, reveling in his pivotal position in the universe and in his creative capacities. Charles Chesneau in his *Le Père Yves de Paris et son temps* says he is sure that Pascal would have objected rather strongly to Yves, for Yves infers God from nature, and Pascal's vacuum experiments are a good example of the reasons Pascal had for thinking that God's existence could not be inferred from nature.[30] But although Chesneau himself points out that Yves is a neo-Platonist, he does not draw attention to the fact that Pascal's objections based on particular facts, powerful as they might be against some natural theologies, would not hold against Yves' positions.

The claim is not that there are particular states of affairs that lead us to infer God, but that God—or the One or the Ultimate Unity—is clearly manifest in each individual thing in so far as that thing is regarded as intelligible. Yves would admit as much as Pascal that the *"raisons sensibles"* will not suffice, but he would insist that the *"raisons moralles"* would suffice.

Pascal, once again, would reply that this Unity is a god of the philosophers and in no sense the "God of Abraham and Isaac," but Yves might respond that, while that might be so if the "God of Abraham and Isaac" is taken literally, the God he is talking about is genuinely our partner in the world. He expresses himself in and through us and, literally, according to Christian doctrine, came to earth as a man. All our creative efforts involve this partnership.

The claim of Yves is not, I think, that we know this for certain, but that the intellect suggests this thesis as the basis of intelligibility. If reality is intelligible in this way—and Yves would say in this way only—is this not the basis for a wager? Yves thinks the case is strong. Yves does not talk of bets. In his own view, there is hardly need for a wager. The outcome is quite certain. But *we* might easily think that Yves overestimates his case while still holding that what he is saying *does* lay the *foundation* for a plausible wager.

Certainly, if my reading is right, this still would not satisfy Pascal. What is at the back of Pascal's claims is the belief that the issue is neither primarily one of rational interest nor of intellectual probability, but rather a moral matter.

But Yves might have something to say in response to this claim also. According to Yves, moral matters do, indeed, arise in this context. But what is expected of human beings is not so difficult to ascertain. We, like everything else, are a product of the law of contraries.

We add a new dimension of freedom and rationality to the universe.[31] God is free as well. But God's freedom essentially pertains to acts considered in terms of their own natures and not in terms of outside interference. That is, God's freedom is expressed through actions natural to the things through which they are expressed. If God creates a stone, his freedom is expressed through the fact that the stone behaves like a stone—for that is the nature he gave it. He does not need to make it behave strangely in order to express his freedom. In a sense it is *necessary* that stones should behave like stones, for otherwise they would be something else. God's necessity in this sense is properly a liberty, Yves says.[32] In the same way, it is necessary for God's goodness to express itself in good deeds and good things, for that is what goodness is. This is not a restriction on God but an expression of his absolute liberty to express his real nature. We are rational like God, but we are unlike God in that our rationality and freedom imply a choice. For the unity to manifest itself in particular beings, each of these beings must be distinguished from other elements in the world. Thus our rationality enables us to think freely because our minds are not already filled with all the possibilities. A negation in us renders us free in a different sense.

We are, therefore, capable of sin, but equally, we are capable of cooperating with God, and each of us has his or her special function to perform. This combination of emphasis on a cooperating stable community and individual responsibility was surely a significant part of Yves' attraction for the bourgeoisie.[33]

Pascal and his Jansenist friends would have worried at the suggestion that one might play a crucial—perhaps even decisive—role in one's own salvation. An evident difficulty in Yves' thesis concerns the distinction between us and God. If we help to save ourselves we play a part of God's role.

The developing Cartesian school provided the strongest rivals to philosophers such as Yves. But they were preceded by Eustachius a Sancto Paulo. Eustachius was a Feuillant monk whose name before he joined the order was Eustache Asseline. He was a moderate who acted as a consultant on monastic reform. The "glorious century" in France caused some people to celebrate human achievements, but others worried about human corruption. Both feelings spurred movements of monastic reform. Angélique Arnauld, the abbess of Port-Royal, consulted Eustachius.

Eustachius was an acute thinker. Descartes read him and in a letter to Marin Mersenne proclaimed him the best of the then surviving scholastic philosophers.[34] Descartes planned, for a time, to add his own notes to Eustachius' manual of philosophy and to publish the result, although whether he meant only to refute Eustachius ("the best" of the scholastics) or also intended to make use of some his ideas, we do not know. Eustachius wrote extensively in metaphysics, physics, and ethics; his religious meditations, though very different in content, show a pattern not unlike that of Descartes' philosophical meditations. His notion of absolute substance and of the power of God to produce the principles that we find in things may be a source of Descartes' own views, and he tried to face head-on the intellectual roots of the problem so worrying to Pascal—the problem of the relation between the sensible and the intelligible.[35] When Pascal proposes a wager, he is making a specific response to this problem, for again, the issue is how the intelligible—the intellectual order—is to manifest itself in the order within which sensory knowledge appears.

The growing gap between what can be known of God and what would have to be known for us to know of the existence of the "God of Abraham and Isaac" is illustrated by the interaction between the ideas of Eustachius and those of Descartes. Eustachius became concerned, inevitably, with the problem of integrating the newer knowledge, the great flood of what we now usually call science, into the traditional theological view of the world.

Based on the view that the new scientists seemed to be promoting, we obviously do not, in some sense, know enough about the world itself to be able to make the kinds of inferences that gave traditional natural theologies their plausibility. The things we know seem to be more closely associated with the human mind than with the objects themselves. Descartes noticed that the so-called secondary qualities—colors, sounds, tastes, smells, and so forth—seem to vary with the observer in a way that suggests that they are not, in and of themselves, in actual things. Malebranche later went a step further to claim that neither primary nor secondary qualities were in things. Eustachius, whose writing begins a generation before Descartes and ends just as Descartes is beginning to write, so that Descartes read him before he wrote the *Méditations,* took a related but slightly different tack, although one that Descartes recognized as perhaps useful for solving the problem of transubstantiation. Working from an older scholastic tradition, he asked about the point at which the perceiving senses and perceived object meet: the surfaces of things.[36]

"La superficie," as Descartes and others called it,[37] was curious. The surface does not actually occupy any space. It therefore can be in the mind and in the thing at the same time. The problem that transubstantiation presents is that one and the same thing is both bread and the body of Christ and wine and the blood of Christ. This problem is seriously compounded by certain elements of Cartesian philosophy, especially by the fact that there is only one "absolute substance." The traditional view is that the appearances remain the same, but the substances change. The *"superficie"* thesis, however, allows one to believe that two things can legitimately occupy the same space because neither actually excludes the other. What this means is that it may be in the nature of the object to occupy space as we see it and also to occupy space at the same time in the different way suggested by physics. In this case, our ideas of things would be compounded of these different ways for the self-expression of things. Our understanding grasps a thing that can be (properly) interpreted in two different ways.

But transubstantiation was not the main issue. In the Eustachian philosophy there is a potential solution to the much-advertised Cartesian problem about mind-body interaction. Descartes appears to have believed that the complaints that he could not solve the mind-body problem arose from a misunderstanding of his philosophy. There is an epistemological issue and an ontological issue. From the point of view of the Cartesian theory of knowledge, the problem is not one of mind-body interaction but one about the relation of different kinds of ideas. Because things are represented by radically different kinds of ideas, it does not necessarily follow that their ontological nature is such as to prevent interaction.

What one might make of Eustachius' claim, however, is that a certain thing has the property of being perceptible as being red and also as being an emitter and absorber of light rays in certain spectrums. As a physical object it is no color at all. As a perceptible object it is red. The redness in this view is really there on the surface of the thing and so is the physical property that we associate with it.

If this were true, we should expect to find what we do find, namely, that there is a more or less constant conjunction between the perception of things as red and the physical data concerning light rays. What kinds of things are intelligible in this way and have sets of properties of the sort described? Eustachius does not pursue this problem, but rather suggests that these different manifestations are manifestations of one substance. If substance is not itself a quality and if any substance can have any quality, then evidently the problem of the apparent incompatibility of qualities does not matter, especially if one has a doctrine of *"la superficie,"* which allows for this incompatibility.

But if substance is wholly distinct from quality, what is it? A substance is whatever is not in another thing, not itself a quality, and finally, is "incommunicable" (i.e., it cannot be passed on from one thing to another). This brings Eustachius to the notion there is only one absolute substance, for everything else exists in and through something else in so far as it has causes and can be given explanations. We clearly cannot know much about this substance except that it is and that it explains all other things. Suppose we accept that there must be such a substance, for surely qualities cannot just exist on their own. Still, such a substance is, at best, the philosopher's god and not the God of "Abraham and Isaac."

Nevertheless, Eustachius also suggests that the truth in things is the transcendental truth that exists in the mind of God and is expressed through the principles of the world as they apply to particular things. His discussion of the traditional notions of the agent and passive intellect suggest that particular things do not literally contain their own principles but that they are what they are because principles—ultimately those of the mind of God—are expressed through them. If so, then the one substance expresses itself through two distinct orders and this gives a further account of how they might be related.[38]

The standard account of Descartes' version of this situation leaves substantially less room for maneuver. According to this version, we are trapped in our own private experience, and if we do not know that God exists, we have no way of determining the truth about the world outside us. In this predicament, our only claim to trustworthy knowledge is that God exists and will not organize our experience so as to deceive us. Such a view does not even include Eustachius' window on reality, and indeed, if we think about own minds we come to the conclusion that mind and matter are mutually exclusive. Mind occupies no space; matter has extension for its essence. This is because, first, the primary qualities on which physical explanation seems to depend have to do with the occupancy of space, but thinking can be understood without any reference to space.

This "common Cartesianism" is probably not what Descartes had in mind, but his successors did not pursue the ideas one might find in Eustachius. They took Descartes' two protosubstances, mind and matter, as ultimate—and they became embroiled in an endless dispute over mind-matter interaction.

But even if one could remain within the ambit suggested by Eustachius, the existence of the one substance (God) would still be necessary to explain the trustworthiness of our experience. Thus, Pascal's problem would seem to remain. The notion that there is an ultimate explanation that we can attain depends on the claims that (1) God (the one substance) exists, (2) God is trustworthy, and (3) God has created us and the world so that we can reason successfully.

Such a God will still be cut off from us because he is an arbitrary creator and is, by his infinity, so different from us as to be unintelligible. Descartes thought that such a being could be proved to exist primarily by two arguments: a form of the ontological argument and the argument that ideas, including the idea of God, have causes. But the first argument is vitiated by the claim that God, if he exists, is the arbitrary creator of the laws of logic. This means, presumably, that if God does not exist the laws of logic are still arbitrary. Perhaps then, the laws of logic just make it seem that God exists when he does not. The second argument shares with the claim that the world is intelligible the difficulty that it depends on the existence of God, thus locking us once more into the Cartesian circle. Descartes puts some stock in a third argument to the effect that one thing I *can* know is that I am a limited and finite creature and that, therefore, I am not the author of my own being. But Pascal naturally complains that this is just the problem: My finite nature creates the infinite distance between me and God and thus makes God unintelligible to me.[39]

2.3 Pascal's Line of Sight

Where does this leave Pascal?

Eustachius and the Cartesians could not, in Pascal's view, close the gap between humanity and God. Philosophers such as Yves de Paris seem to Pascal to close it too easily. They believe that, in ourselves, we are nothing, yet our being follows from God's use of the principle of contrariety. We exist, as it were, by excluding other things. And Bérulle, too, believes that we exist thanks to the various emanations of God—that God overcomes our nothingness through the nature of his own being. To enable us to return to God from a nature in which he leaves inadequate traces of himself, Malebranche and Yves-Marie André build this picture, step-by-step, into a kind of cooperation between us and God. We have a measure of being of our own because God seeks to realize possibilities that he must realize through our freedom.

God takes, if you like, bets on us.

Yet the Malebranche-André analysis would also give a reason for making the bet that Pascal proposes—the bet that the world can be made to make sense in these terms and that, if such a God exists, he works with us and through us. He bets on us.

One must not simply suppose that Pascal would oppose these doctrines. For, although he frequently makes much of the "infinite distance" that separates God from us, he also frequently speaks in various ways as well of the *union* of humanity and God.[40] God would, of course, have been infinitely distant from us in a way that would have made communication hopeless had not he, himself, intervened—especially in the Incarnation. Pascal's equal emphasis on the unity of God and humanity and on the infinite distance between them is simply a central part of his argument for Christianity, which he takes to be the only religion that makes this relation clear. (He seems not to have known or not to have thought about the Krishnaite version of Hinduism.)

What Pascal is worried about, however, is the possibility that the world cannot really be made to make sense by any philosophical argument. But his reasons for this are *moral*. Human beings, he says, in the full knowledge of one, himself, caught up in the scientific revolution of the time, have unbelievable capacities and possibilities. Yet the world seems to be very bad.

His objection, I think, to the implication that he no doubt senses in the neo-Platonists of his time, such as Yves de Paris and Bérulle, is exactly that they *do* make sense of a world that is very bad. This, of course, is partly a reflection of the fact that the physical world is also devoid of divine traces.

Yet if Pascal is right about how bad the world is, would there be any sense in betting at all?

Pascal seems to come very near to and yet end very far from his neo-Platonist contemporaries. This is the problem that I now examine by exploring the doctrine of the three orders.

3

The Doctrine of Orders

3.1 The Three Orders and the Human Predicament

PASCAL DESCRIBED A WORLD THAT CAN BE DIVIDED INTO THREE REALMS OR orders. There is the realm of physical objects, the realm of ideas, and the moral realm. He believed that God, if he exists and is infinite, must manifest himself in each of the three realms.

In a sense, it is literally true that these three orders are three *distinct* realms.[1] Each of the realms reflects some aspect of the essence of an infinite being—an aspect appropriate to that realm.

We know fairly straightforwardly what it is to exist in the physical order. Pascal's account of the point that moves at infinite velocity and is therefore everywhere at once shows how he thinks it is possible even for God to exist in such a realm.[2]

To exist in the intellectual realm is to exist after the manner of an idea. Thus we might say that the number two exists in the number system. But Pascal means more than this, for the ideas he is thinking of help give intelligibility to the world; they are principles that underlie all orders including the physical order, and they must inform the world, not merely exist in a Platonic heaven even if, as he said in the letter to Mme Périer, our position is like that of the denizens of Plato's cave.[3]

How the order of charity, the moral order, has its being is a more difficult matter. It is associated with the order presided over by the form of the good itself, but if one merely considers this aspect of it, it would not be clearly separated from the intellectual order. It is manifested, rather, through the principles that properly animate those who really know. In so far as human beings are properly human, they are capable of knowing and instantiating these principles; but in so far as they are fallen creatures far from the heart of this order, they are lost and struggle against the principles. Their condition is that of the opening words of the wager fragment—*"infini rien."* They are infinite because they could, in principle, at least if they are not "fallen," know everything. But they are nothing because if one asks what a human being is, the answers quickly dissolve. In the physical realm, human beings are constituted of matter that has formed many bodies in the past and will later form many more. In the intellectual order is there really an idea of the human being? Pascal says it is the idea of a "thinking reed."[4] The human being is nothing in itself. Only in the moral order can the human being, as agent, realize its real nature. We must think of ourselves as "neither angel nor beast."[5] We are poised between the realms, precisely as a kind of bridge between the angels and the beasts, and "our nature is to be in motion."[6] Ultimately, though, the nature of the human being (in the sense of the driving force) "is altogether animal, he is all animal."[7]

Yet one must be careful. Pascal is *not* offering a tripartite distinction, two parts of which correspond to Descartes' finite quasi-substances of mind and matter and which, in turn, can be thought of in terms of our knowledge of them as the introspectable and the measurable. Nor is the problem of relating them, for Pascal, simply or mainly a matter of relating kinds of knowledge.

Even if, as many readers have thought, for Descartes the distinctions between mind and matter involve very deep ontological breaks, they are not distinctions that create fundamental problems about human action. Based on the Cartesian view, our legitimate concerns about mind and matter are intellectual. The moral realm hardly intrudes as a serious "third order." But for Pascal, all problems center on questions about what we ought to do.

Nor would Pascal begin like Locke by making primary the notion that there are different fundamental kinds of knowledge. His ontology and epistemology are closer to Locke's than to Descartes', but the context is different. Locke *does* admit there is real moral knowledge and even says that it is like mathematics.[8] Intelligibility somehow radiates from God (whose existence, Locke says, is the basis of knowledge[9]) to inform the whole range of the intellectual, the physical, and the moral. But Pascal is worried about the ultimate intelligibility of the world to us, given that we are poised between the infinite and the nothing and must make our own way.

For Pascal, the fragmentation of the world is very real in a way that poses insurmountable problems for us. We can grasp moral principles, but our world is so fragmented that we do not really know, without divine guidance, how to apply them. Our mathematical powers are enormous. But the connection between mathematics and physical reality is extremely obscure. We have a good deal of success in applying mathematics to physics; yet the necessities and the intuitive certainties that apply to mathematics are absent from physics. Even in the domain of mathematics itself, when we come to infinities, we become puzzled. It runs against our intuition to think that infinity plus one is the same number as infinity, and that both are equal to infinity minus one.

To a mathematician such as Pascal, it must have been tempting to think that there is something suggesting the hand of God in the fact that mathematics does work in nature—just as in our own time Sir Arthur Eddington reckoned that it must be true that God mathematicizes.[10] In the preceding chapter, I showed that Pascal thought mathematics our best hope of knowledge of the world. Ultimately, however, it fails.[11]

I also discussed the importance that Pascal attached to the idea of the infinite. Pascal thinks the relation of the finite to the infinite tends to undermine our claims about knowledge of the world. If we were to have clear expressions of our relation to God, we would have, as Pascal says in the wager fragment,[12] a clear idea of the relation of infinite to finite quantities.

The vacuum experiments, which show the apparent omnipresence of things to be due simply to air pressure, did not, however, simply teach Pascal that one could not infer directly from physical reality to God. They also helped to persuade him that the three orders must be kept separate.

One can show that God is a possibility within the physical realm.[13] But even if one adds this possibility to the "idea of God" that exists in the intellectual realm and also takes account of the moral realm and the principles of goodness that animate the order of charity, one is still at sea. We are confused and see, not through a glass darkly, but through three different modes of thought and enquiry. Still, we are not actually in the position of the Pyrrhonist of whom Pascal often speaks.

The classical skeptic may have been disturbed by the urge to believe and puzzled about how to conduct practical life. Yet such a skeptic had, in principle, no strong predilection toward one belief rather than another and so did not have the problem that troubles the prospective Christian. Nonetheless, we are also not in the position of fideistic skeptics such as La Mothe le Vayer,[14] who suppose that—in *some* matters—one is quite free to believe anything whatever and therefore can combine skepticism in science with strong belief in a religion that might be irrational. Pascal claims that we do have *intellectual* intimations of God in each of the realms and that these intimations are truly disquieting. We have a strong sense that there really are moral principles. But when we settle down to apply them rationally, we are apt to finish in the predicament of the seventeenth-century Jesuits, for the rules tend to conflict.

We do have powerful metaphysical arguments, but Pascal supposes them to be useless outside the purely intellectual realm. Yet Descartes himself, says Pascal, is not merely useless, he is also *troublesome*.[15] He provides disquieting (and muddling) hints of the existence of God. Even the physical realm is not wholly immune to disquieting signs of the existence of God; there are the reports of the Incarnation and continuing reports of miracles. Even if their credibility is doubtful, Pascal finds such reports troubling precisely because they raise questions about the capacity of human beings to believe and about how such things can be conceivable.[16]

3.2 The Basis of the Three Orders

Faced with a fragmented world that is confusing but nonetheless full of hints and intimations of God, the Pascalian must try to come to grips with the human situation. To show how Pascal manages, I now examine the basis of the doctrine of the three orders.

Pascal was no Cartesian, yet the notion of the three orders can be seen as a way of reflecting on Cartesianism. Descartes himself did not see the mind-body problem as very threatening to his philosophy, for he did not see it in the way that many of his readers did. Mind and matter are admittedly distinct *apparent* substances, but there is only one absolute (infinite) substance in Descartes' system. Certainly, again, there are different kinds of ideas with different kinds of relations to reality, but they all derive their being from a single absolute substance. All natural and logical laws are, in any case, for a strict Cartesian simply the arbitrary creations of God—and God can organize the world as he pleases. Although Descartes expected continued rationality and efficiency from God, he did not, within those limits, think that any one mode of organization is intrinsically more surprising than another. He assured one of his correspondents, Princess Elizabeth of Bohemia, that although he wrote the *Meditations* to show the distinctness of mind from matter by way of illustrating the kinds of ideas, he might have written another work to show their connection.[17]

It happens, Descartes argues, that the idea of myself as a thinking thing is an idea that cannot exist unless its object also exists, whereas the idea of a mountain or the idea of an old shoe can readily exist when its object does not. Whether thinking things and old shoes interact depends on the kinds of causal laws that relate things.

In the Cartesian philosophy, there is no reason why different kinds of things should not form part of a law-governed system. Descartes himself had hoped to build his picture of the physical world out of the concept of extension, and many of his followers who read him as holding that there are two ultimate and distinct substances wanted a kind of push-and-pull system that a two-substance thesis cannot easily accommodate.

Pascal surely began from some distinctions like those Descartes was inclined to make, but he went in a wholly different direction from that taken by Descartes' followers. Human beings, he thought, are clearly aware of at least three systems in which every human being takes part. The system of the body, the physical order, is complete in itself. Science can approach all of human experience. When the scientific system seems to lead beyond itself, the seeming is always an illusion.

All signs of "design" that the mind finds in the world turn out to be misunderstandings of one kind or another. Nevertheless, there is an order of the intellect, for we know that it is "absurd to say that inanimate bodies have passions, fears, hatreds."[18] Pascal does not mean by this that brains are not involved in thinking or that there could not be intelligent machines. He has, after all, a better claim than anyone else to be considered the inventor of what people now call the "intelligent machine."[19] And in the *Pensées,* he tells us that this machine approaches nearer to thought than "anything done by animals."[20]

Yet "nearer to thought" is not thought, and he insists that "it [the machine] has no will." In any case, one cannot get "one little thought" from all the bodies in the world.[21] Thinking, for Pascal, is closely tied to believing, and believing is related to the will, so the absence of will in calculating machines is fatal to claims that they think.

He means, to put it differently, that matter does not give rise to what are often, nowadays, called propositional attitudes. Matter does not believe or disbelieve in the existence of God. If machines indicate that some propositions are "true," they simply show that these propositions follow from some premises or arise under some conditions they have been programmed to accept. They do not find propositions meaningful or meaningless except in the sense that some propositions conform to criteria they have been programmed to accept—whereas a human being can conceive of a proposition as being meaningful and yet not conforming to any criterion previously given. (Think of a man or a woman reading *Finnegans Wake.*)

And do machines understand? The critical sense and the creative element in knowledge alike demand a distinction between automatic actions and thinking. And so there *is* an intellectual order.

Descartes noticed that one cannot easily go from this intellectual order to proof of the existence of the physical order. And this fact is far more important than anything that might follow from the "causal" distinctions between mind and matter. Descartes believed that the intellectual order contains the necessary materials for the proof of the existence of God—that is, that the existence of God follows solely from the idea of God—and that one can then demonstrate the existence of the physical world from experience combined with the proposition that God would not deceive us.

Pascal says that the proofs for the existence of God are simply too complicated.[22] Most of all, they do not move us. They hold our attention only for the hour when we study them. In one sense they are not even sound. They locate God only in the intellectual order in which the proofs begin.

When Pascal says in the same passage that the proofs are "without Jesus Christ," what does he mean? They may apply to God the father, but they do not apply to or move us in the worlds in which Jesus operated—the physical world and the world of the moral order. Just as the physical order does not lead us beyond itself when we study it, so the intellectual order seems closed in on itself and not able to lead beyond itself.

If one accepts that Pascal's concerns are primarily moral, one sees at once a further and very important difficulty for Pascal as he addresses Descartes. Descartes' proofs start in the intellectual order but they use the intellectual order to infer something about the moral order. Descartes insists that we can have knowledge because God exists and is trustworthy.

As Pascal records his response to Descartes, it may seem that two of the *Pensées* contradict each other. In one, Pascal says that Descartes is "useless";[23] in the other, he says that the metaphysical proofs are merely complicated and do not move us.[24] But there need be no contradiction. Descartes admits the existence of two worlds—the physical and the moral. But his argument does not take him into the moral order.

The intellectual God who figures in the proofs from the idea of God is that being whose idea is necessary in the intellectual order. That is, we cannot think away the idea of God. But is he trustworthy? No such question arises in the intellectual world where relations are purely logical. Does he then guarantee the existence of the physical world? Not if he is simply an intellectual being. (Descartes knows this and allows that God might even change the laws of logic; no doubt he could change the physical laws as well.)

Descartes certainly does care about the trustworthiness of God. Trustworthiness is an issue that arises in our world. We know that moral beings can be trusted because it is the nature of the moral order that it transcends self-interest. Pascal does not provide an argument for such a claim but rather asks us to examine our own moral lives.

What he keeps saying throughout the *Pensées* is that moral issues do confront us. Sometimes he would have liked it otherwise. He would have liked not to have to trouble his conscience about whether he should encourage his sister Jacqueline to take part of their inheritance to live at Port-Royal. He might well have said that no moral questions arise so long as one can stick to self-interest.

One would then be in a different order of things. Morality arises as an issue only when self-interest must be constrained. Pascal's whole notion of the human condition is predicated on the fact that the "fall of man" creates a predicament. Our progenitors wanted to know the difference between good and evil. They wanted to make their own decisions about it. But the difference between good and evil is the difference between what is good for all and can be shared by all and what is good for the individual but cannot be shared. Hence the self-assertion involved in our desire to make our own decisions at once pits us against morality. To reach this order, therefore, we must reach beyond the physical and intellectual orders because our knowledge of these orders is tied to our own perspectives.

But how *does* one reach the moral order? There are two apparent possibilities in Pascal's writings. Based on one reading, Pascal believes that it is only through an act of religious faith that one can reach the moral order at all. Hence, one who bets on the existence of God commits himself, inevitably, to behave morally toward others, for salvation depends on treating the saved as if they were saved, and one does not know who is saved and who is not. Therefore one should treat everyone as if he or she were saved. But this makes morality, once again, a kind of pragmatic exhibition of self-interest. Treat others as if they were saved so that you yourself may be saved. Such exhibitions of self-interest are precisely not what is required in the realm of morality.

The other reading suggests that our knowledge of morality leads us to a position in which one must bet on the existence of God. We do, in fact, have a sense of the moral world. But because we do, we would think that a natural knowledge of morality must precede theological knowledge or even religious conviction. Pascal seems to insist on the priority of religious knowledge. Accordingly, it is often argued, for instance by A. W. S. Baird,[25] that Pascal's attitude to "natural morality" is "ambivalent."

A reader of the *Lettres Provinciales* who followed all the attacks on Jesuit moral theory would surely conclude that Pascal is downright hostile to natural morality. But there is a basic ambiguity about this hostility. Pascal is hostile to morality based on the facts about our "natures" within the physical and intellectual realms, as well as to the Jesuit practice of accepting various excuses based on particular worldly circumstances. The moral realm is constituted of moral ideas, and what is "natural" to it could not be anything other than genuine morality. It forces itself on our experience, however, not through our sensory experience nor, strictly speaking, through our reason, for sensation belongs to the physical realm, and reason, in and of itself, to the intellectual realm.

How, then, can we reach the moral realm? The answer is that we are aware of the incompleteness and relative unreality of the other two realms. Pascal thinks that we are aware of this precisely in the way one might expect. It is clear to us that our natural ends are not given to us either by our knowledge of the physical realm or by our knowledge of the intellectual realm. No thought can be found in the physical realm, and knowledge of ends must be something found through thought. Yet reason can be used for any end whatsoever. Therefore, there is a lack. The grandeur of the human condition and its poverty alike testify to some enormous end toward which we are driven. Wherever we look and however we think about the human condition, we can scarcely avoid thinking about the principles of conduct, and we can scarcely avoid the thesis that the source of such principles must be beyond the realms of the purely physical and the purely intellectual.

As Kant was to argue a century later, there is a natural independence to morals.

Lucien Goldmann makes much of the similarity between Kant's categorical imperative and Pascal's belief that we must act as if all men and women were saved.[26] Why must we treat all human beings in this way? Pascal says that we do not know who is saved and who is damned, and this is crucial.[27] He obviously believes that God intends us to treat the saved as if they were saved. Treating the damned as damned is something best left to God. But because we do not know who they are, the only way to avoid disastrous mistakes is to treat them all as saved.

More fundamentally, perhaps, Pascal is convinced that the only thing that counts as a proper end for human beings is something that transcends both the physical and the intellectual. But what transcends both of these is necessarily something that cannot be the special possession of any single man or woman. For it to be such a special possession, it would have to be something in the realm in which we are individuated—essentially in the physical realm. Even if it were in the intellectual realm in some way or other, it could be so only in some way attached to sentiments of individual possession. Morality leads us to the universal.

Goldmann makes a connection between Pascal's formulation and the first form of Kant's categorical imperative—act always in such a way that you can will your act to become a universal law. But Pascal is thinking of a human community with a common aim, and the connection is therefore even stronger if one thinks of Kant's "Kingdom of Ends" formulation: Act always, says Kant, as if you and all others were members of the Kingdom of Ends. The Kingdom of Ends is the kingdom of the saved seen from the perspective of moral obligation. It is that kingdom within which each person is seen to be an end in him or herself. In substantive terms, it is a society in which each is necessary to the well being of all and where, therefore, everyone understands the necessity of honoring the natural desire that every other rational and sentient being has to achieve his or her own natural end. Pascal would want to deny that we are necessary to God in the way that God is necessary to us. And yet we are, he would insist, necessary parts of God's plan for the world, for he chooses for the best and has chosen to include us.

Emphasizing his neo-Platonism, Pascal insists that we are, indeed, "members" of God.[28] Unless, therefore, we achieve whatever end God has planned for us, God's plan will fail. Such a failure is unthinkable, for we are God's "members" in the sense that our hands and feet are "our members." But it is unthinkable only because God will accord us whatever grace must be accorded in order for his plan to succeed.

The notion that we are "members" of God leads the argument along strange but profound lines. It means, in part, that God's existence in the moral order is expressed through us. If God does exist, his plan can be fulfilled only through us, and we are free creatures. The same principles that animate God animate us.

But suppose God does not exist in the moral realm? Then in what sense does he not exist? Only in the sense that the moral principles are not instantiated in the world. If we all behave well, will it not be as if God existed? And if we all behave as if we are saved and this makes for a good world, will not this—from the perspective of the *moral* realm—even be the same as being saved?

This leads, once again, to the argument I have been claiming all along is at the heart of Pascal's thinking: The wager is justified because we can see that, morally, in any case, we must behave as if God existed, for it is Pascal's specific argument that you would be entitled to behave to people as if they were not saved only if, in fact, you knew they were damned. But you cannot know this because God, if he exists, has not told you. But equally—and this is sometimes forgotten by those who write about Pascal—if God does not exist, he *cannot* tell us who is saved and who is not.

Therefore, we have nothing to lose by believing that God exists. The existence of God in the full sense is still not a certainty. But it is not a certainty only because God, if he exists at all, must exist in the intellectual and the *physical* realms as well as in the moral realm.

3.3 The Special Problem of the Natural World

There is still something very unsatisfying about the whole argument to this point. The argument now seems to pivot on the moral issue. Urging us to bet on the existence of God in these terms is a way of telling us to behave well. But the infinite gains of which Pascal speaks seem to be associated chiefly with the much vaguer notions of the God who exists in the intellectual realm and who could, just possibly, exist in the physical realm as the point that moves at infinite velocity and is therefore everywhere at once.[29]

Pascal's situation among the Platonized Augustinians at Port-Royal and his own declarations in many passages and in the letter of 1 April 1648, which he and Jacqueline sent to their sister Mme Périer, all lead one to suppose that these notions can be made to fit together in the way that I suggest at the beginning of this chapter. They make, that is, a kind of neo-Platonism. But we need more details.

Remember the situation. We are asked to bet that there is a supreme being who exists in all three orders. This being appears, if at all, in different forms: in the physical order, it is the point moving at infinite velocity; in the intellectual order, it is Descartes' God-as-necessary idea; in the moral order, it is the principle underlying the Kingdom of Ends—a principle that tends to give form to the other orders and that, above all, defines what we ought to do as human beings. We are also asked to believe that this God may save us or damn us, that believing in his existence will have some influence on this decision, and that believing in his existence is not only consistent with the claims of the moral order but helps to complete that order.

We need more structure. Some scholars steeped in Pascal's work naturally enough leap to the notion that some sort of Platonism is involved, but equally naturally, they do not quite agree about what kind. For instance, Jacques Chevalier is inclined to ascribe to Pascal a literal Platonism straight out of the *Republic*,[30] but A. W. S. Baird, after discussing this possibility, concludes that what is involved is an Augustinian neo-Platonism.[31] Henri Gouhier, by contrast, is more careful about the ascription of Platonism.[32]

One can see Gouhier's point if one realizes that those of us who support the Platonist reading of Pascal face a serious problem: If Pascal were a Platonist in any of the most straightforward senses, one would begin to wonder why the wager should arise at all. Once God is established in the moral realm, the moral realm is associated with the form of the good, and the form of the good is associated with the basic explanation for the whole state of the universe. Even the uncertainty about whether God exists in the physical realm as an actuality or merely as a latent possibility would seem to vanish.

Surely the natural theology of Yves de Paris or one like it, easily available to Pascal in the Paris of the hour, would suffice and, indeed, would form a far better and clearer basis for an apology. To get an answer to this quite crucial puzzle, I shall examine closely what Pascal actually says about the positions adopted in the *Pensées*.

In the letter to Mme Périer, Pascal (along with his sister Jacqueline) speaks of how invisible things are "represented by" visible ones and of how God thereby allows us a glimpse of what we lost in the Fall. The doctrine he puts forward is something like this: There are several ways of "reading" our experience. The contents of our sensations can be taken, in one way, to be simply what they seem to be. We can regard what they seem to be either from the perspective of our own perceptions and take them to be just colored patches, sounds, smells, or whatever; or we can take them to be literally the objects in the outside world that common sense takes them to be. In this sense they are material objects. Beyond both of these possibilities we can intellectualize them. If we count them, they stand as markers for numbers. This is the simplest sense of the visible representing the invisible. The number six cannot be "seen," but it can be "represented" by six things that can be seen. Indeed, the Greeks commonly "represented" numbers by physical objects in just this way. Finally, we can apply these intellectualizations to the given objects of experience, getting, if you like, the basis of mathematical physics. This gives us our first glimpse of the reality underlying our sensory experience.

We do not, however, simply ask the questions that physicists ask about the objects of our awareness. We can, and do, ask what they are "good for." The things and ideas of which we are aware can be used for ends we choose in the physical and the intellectual realms. This obviously does not exhaust our questions. If things and ideas can be *used* by us for our own ends, is it not possible that they have value in and of themselves or for some end that is not that of any particular human being? If we see the virtues of things in and of themselves we begin to see virtue not merely in relation to our ends but as valuable in itself, as least as virtue in itself might be expressed through particular things. In this way we begin to see how, by asking questions about the actual contents of our experience and by making a series of distinctions, we may begin to understand such a Platonism not as a distant abstraction but as a response to issues that arise within our experience.

Though Pascal's thesis is a variant of Platonism in so far as it leads us from the immediacies of sensory experience to an underlying more fundamental structure that has affinities with traditional notions of Platonic idealism, it is not quite what we usually think of as Platonism. It has, however, a resemblance to some other views developed in the period. For instance, the theory of ideas put forth by Pascal can be compared to the one found in some of John Locke's posthumously published writings on Malebranche and John Norris.[33] Locke's account has an evident relation to the theses of the Cambridge Platonists even though it keeps a very great critical distance from them.

According to Locke, what is presented directly to the mind—what Locke calls ideas—must always be interpreted. What is directly presented to us gives us grounds for belief in an objective world, but we must work at the inferences involved. In replying to Norris, Locke finally admits that "ideas may be real beings, though not substances."[34] He means by this that ideas are what is interpreted but not something over and above all their interpretations. To be a material substance is to be the correct interpretation of an idea. What we know is the interpretation, though we may insist as we see the interpretations unfold that the idea is capable of more than one interpretation. Presumably, to insist that the idea is something over and above its interpretations would be like suggesting that a word with several meanings is something over and above all its meanings.

Nor can we, in any simple way, move from what we know of these ideas to something more fundamental to the structure of reality. In analyzing Malebranche, Locke calls attention to what he takes to be an unfounded logical leap— Malebranche's claim that when we really know objects our wills become united with God's.[35] In the *Essay,* Locke presents an argument to show how our very being as moral agents is related to these perceptual and interpretative processes— how, as he puts it, "Moral beings and Notions are founded on and terminated in these simple *Ideas*, we have received from Sensation and Reflection."[36] We are thus left as moral agents to make our own decisions. In making them we come to be active moral agents and thus take our places in the moral order.

Later in the *Essay,* Locke argues that the mere existence of knowledge requires the existence of God.[37] But this is at best arguable, and Locke would insist that, if he is right, this still does not guarantee that our *wills* coincide with God's.

Pascal, while admitting like Locke that we do have some knowledge and while even admitting that the existence of God in the intellectual realm may be demonstrable, does not think that the chain of reasoning that unfolds the structure of our ideas will lead us to the existence of God in the full sense. Indeed, it is precisely Pascal's view that the very process that leads us to recognize our being as moral agents in the full sense leads to the situation in which we must bet. His account of "the Fall" is always that the Fall led to a "hateful self," to self-centeredness and to the concupiscence that "is our second nature."[38] But this happened because we sought the knowledge of good and evil. The biblical account has it that we ate the fruit of the very tree of the knowledge of good and evil. In so doing we became in a measure self-creating beings. For, strictly speaking, created things have God's knowledge of good and evil built into them. They are able to act from their own natures without choosing and so are either beasts or angels. Pascal insists that human beings are neither.[39]

This striving for moral knowledge was thus the original and great human gamble. In demanding to choose, we have made all nature our own nature and so hang poised between infinity and nothing. Ideally, perhaps, as Pascal says, we are a mean between infinity and nothing, but nonetheless we are poised between them.[40]

But we cannot manage it by ourselves. The task is too immense, Pascal thinks. We need God's cooperation even if we reject his imposition of good and evil upon us. This is really why we must bet.

Of course, the availability of invisible things (ideas) that can serve to represent visible things would make the notion of a God who is real but not apparent more plausible. If one went further still and developed a doctrine of idea that amounted to a full-blooded Platonism, one might even seem to make the wager unnecessary. At least, as I argue in chapter 5, a more full-blooded Platonism would lead to a different wager. But Pascal's Platonism seems to tie the ideas available to us rather closely to immediate experience, and the doctrine of ideas he espouses *might* amount to little more than the ideas whose reality Locke rather grudgingly admits in his response to Norris. In Pascal's view, our situation is one in which our knowledge must fall far short of certainty.

What has to be seen is that it is both true that there is *some* foundation for the view that a kind of Platonism is to be found in Pascal and that the wager remains necessary to him. *Ideas (idées)* is mentioned seventeen times in the *Pensées.* In some fragments, "idea" only means "opinion," and in others, minor aspects of Cartesian ideas are mentioned. But the *pensées* in which Pascal speaks of "idea" in a philosophical sense as something important in his thinking seem always to give the term a Platonic aspect, however limited.

In grasping what is at issue here, a long fragment on *"les pyrrhoniens"* (which I mentioned earlier) is as important for the present enquiry as the letter to Mme Périer. In this fragment Pascal makes the point that "nature confounds the Pyrrhonists and reason confounds the dogmatists."[41] One might think that Pascal means to call attention to the fact that our nature makes believers of us, and one might think, too, that he is calling attention to the *success* of science as a practical matter. Both claims are true, but they are not the whole story. Pascal thinks there seems to be a way of making our experience intelligible because science is capable of showing how the visible may represent the invisible. In this and other ways nature is constantly giving us hints. These hints pull us away from the skeptics. But reason confounds believers (the dogmatists) because reason can always produce alternatives.

In this same fragment, Pascal says, "What a chimera is man—what an innovation, what a monster, what chaos, what subject of contradiction." He adds that the human being is both the "judge of everything" and "an imbecile earthworm." For a moment his Platonism seems destroyed. Then he says that we do have an idea of happiness—even of beatitude—and we could not have such an idea if we had *always* been corrupt. This is the principal clue to the transcendental goodness—the universal form of goodness and beauty that justifies us in believing that we do have some access to the realm of morality. But *truth* is missing from this list. "We perceive an image of truth, but possess only a lie."

If we do, after all, have some idea of the transcendentals, how is it, then, that we have no idea of truth? Indeed, truth is not just missing from the list. In the same fragment, Pascal asserts bluntly, "We have no idea of truth." This assertion, no doubt, is connected to the fact that we do not have a clear idea about the attainment of bliss or beatitude. Truth and goodness are connected in the same logical way as evil and error. But we do not have a direct idea of the good because we are fallen creatures. Thus we need grace.

The assertion about the absence of the idea of truth occurs in a discussion of sleep and dreaming. Pascal says that we do not know for sure when we are awake and when we are dreaming except by faith. If we really had *"une idée du vrai,"* this problem would not arise, for then we would be able to apply this idea directly. The suggestion, therefore, is that ideas do not provide, *at one move,* a criterion for truth. The simplest account of this impossibility relies on the distinction between formal and objective reality. At least that is the orthodox Cartesian point of view. Here, Pascal seems to agree with Descartes. Knowledge of the forms of things in Pascal's as well as Descartes' accounts of dreaming does not guarantee existence of the things dreamed of. Objective reality, literally, is the power of an idea, or of anything, to refer to something in the world. Not only may dream ideas be instantiated, but they may also lack the power of reference so that we cannot check up on them to see whether or not they do refer. But if we take the whole of our sensory experience, simply *as* our sensory experience, our waking experience is not in any better situation.

Descartes says there are certain ideas—of myself and God—that are so constituted that their formal (actual) and objective realities coincide. But it is important to remember that Pascal does not think that the self, considered as any entity wholly separate from God, really exists, and he also thinks that the *idea* of God leads us only to the God who exists in the *intellectual* realm.

Pascal keeps coming back in different ways to the beginning of the wager fragment: "infinity" and "nothing." The human animal is both. Men and women can encompass everything in thought and in experience, but in themselves they are nothing.

Our best knowledge, mathematical knowledge and the representation of natural orders in physics, does not, after all, pass beyond existence *in intellectu*. In admitting the transcendentals, of course, Pascal sets up the Platonic or neo-Platonic line of argument. But in commenting on our idea of truth, he weakens it again.

What he means to suggest is that the intellect alone is not sufficient to bring us to the truth. Goodness and beauty come through to us, but they do so, after all, in a fallen world. They are not fully instantiated—or even fully instantiable—by us in this world. But our intellects and our senses are tied to this world. One might interpret this in two ways. The first is simply to hold that Pascal means us to abandon this world and seek salvation in the next. The second is to hold that the world must be changed so that truth and goodness are possible to it.

Based on the first view, goodness cannot survive here; truth is beyond this world. But Pascal did not believe any such thing. He spent much of his time during the last painful period of his life creating the first public bus line in Paris. He envisaged it as a service to the poor—who otherwise had to walk and whose poverty was often connected to their lack of mobility. But he also hoped to make money from it that could be used for the benefit of the poor. He actually did so, and his will contains detailed instructions about how profits from the bus system are to be distributed to various hospitals and charitable institutions.[42]

We must then assume that the second interpretation holds: We are supposed to act so as to change the world. This is a gamble. One must wager one's life on it, and indeed, Pascal did. The view that there is no clear idea of truth may seem strange, but Pascal is simply taking a more straightforward reading of a certain part of the Platonic tradition than most philosophers have.

Plato himself held that the chaos of this world never perfectly exhibits the forms, and indeed, that truth really belongs in the realm of the transcendentals, one of the higher regions of the realm of the "forms," and is not in our world. Hence, he has a curious way of distinguishing truth from right opinion. The forms are fully intelligible, but things in the world are not. There is truth about the forms but only right opinion about the things in the ordinary world. Those who have taken this view of Plato, however, have usually thought the illness of the world to be incurable.

Yet such views are paradoxical. If our world cannot be the bearer of truth, how can we know it? Our own minds would have to instantiate truth in order for us to know that it cannot be instantiated. And, if justice is not possible to us, how could we know that this is so? We would have to be able to imagine a just society to which our own society could never measure up. But if we could imagine it, how could we be sure that it could never be instantiated?

In the fragment cited,[43] Pascal tries to escape such paradoxes in the following way: first, goodness and beauty do come through to us. But truth requires their instantiation. What is imperfect cannot be the bearer of truth, for its imperfections involve a kind of disorder through which truth cannot be discerned. Of course, goodness and beauty do not come through to our imperfect intellects but are revealed to us only in so far as we penetrate the moral realm. We grasp them in our moral insights. What we can do, therefore, is to try to act morally. In so doing we can try to transform the world so as to make it the bearer of truth. God watches our struggles and knows that, given our imperfections, we cannot succeed on our own. But in struggling to bring goodness to the world, we create an opening through which God can act if he chooses—an opening, no doubt, for which God has already planned and which is part of his natural universe but not of ours. We do not make the world good, but we act out part of a plan that makes that goodness possible.

This is close to Lucien Goldmann's reading in *Le Dieu caché*, except that it involves a more cooperative relation between humankind and God and preserves Pascal's repeated statements that we cannot really succeed in anything important by ourselves without necessarily implying the kind of "tragic vision" to which Goldmann is committed.

3.4 Getting God into the Physical World

It is still very important that Pascal should be able to fit God into the natural world. In the *Pensées,* the fragment in which he describes how God *might* fit into the world is almost certainly intended to come immediately after the wager fragment itself, and I shall now examine more closely what Pascal says to show what he had in mind.

He says:[44]

Croyez-vous qu'il soit impossible que Dieu soit infini, sans parties? Oui. Je vous veux donc faire voir (une image de Dieu en son immensité) une chose infinie et indivisible: C'est un point (remuant) se mouvant partout d'une vitesse infinie. Car il est—*un*—en tous lieux et est tout entier en chaque endroit.

Do you believe that it would be impossible for God to be infinite and without parts? Yes. I want to let you see an image of the immensity of God: something both infinite and indivisible. It is a moving point which moves everywhere at an infinite speed. Because it is—*one*—everywhere and it is complete in each place.

There are a few curiosities in this text: If "point" is a Euclidian geometrical point, then it is difficult to see how it can move at all. A Euclidean point occupies no space, and there is no way of distinguishing one point from another. Lines are sets of points, but apart from their locations, all points are the same. We must suppose that what Pascal has in mind is something of minimal mass—something whose minimal mass renders it indivisible but that, nonetheless, because it occupies space, can be said to occupy different places at different times. Then, if it moves infinitely fast, it can, indeed, be said to be everywhere at once, for it will take it no time at all to get from A to B.

If such a God can *possibly* exist—that is, if such a God is compatible with what it is reasonable to believe about the natural universe—then Pascal believed that his case should be taken seriously, for we have good reason to believe that God exists in the other two orders, the intellectual and the moral, and all we need to know is that a certain kind of possibility exists in order to have a good reason to *bet* that he exists in the natural order (or world) as well.

It may well seem that God's existence is compatible with any possible physical world. The climate is never too harsh for God. He exists in and of himself and needs no special environment for nourishment. Whatever the physical world is like, one might think, it will make no difference to him. The moral environment is, to be sure, another matter; if God is good and omnipotent, his existence is incompatible with the existence of certain kinds of evil. But here we are concerned with the physical world.

Still, God's seeming compatibility might be deceiving. If God is omnipotent— that is, if he has all logically possible powers—then there are problems. For instance, the power to seem red to one who cannot be deceived about colors (and that is a possible power) can be possessed only by a being who actually is red. To be omnipotent, therefore, one must possess all possible characteristics—and that would not seem to leave any for other things. This is a curiosity. It seems to follow that the characteristic of being an entity wholly other than God is not possible if God is omnipotent. (One must remember that a *possessed* characteristic is always particular; the brownness of Susie's eyes and the brownness of Sally's eyes are both brown, but they are distinct.)

Things in the world are distinguished from one another because some things possess some properties and some possess others. God, in this case, would have all the qualities, and other things would be distinguished by some lack or other. Thus God would overlap with all the things in the world—everything would be what it is and, also in some sense, *part* of God.

This interpretation is simplified by the introduction of the notion of the infinitely fast-moving point; it is everywhere at once, but it is distinguished from other things by its different diversity of temporal and spatial dimensions. This principle can be extended, no doubt, to cover *mutatis mutandis,* the possession of the various characteristics. Furthermore, the omnipotence of God could be extended beyond the normal logical limits of space-dominated worlds. He might—as Descartes would agree—be able to effect causal changes by acting through the past.

If then God, considered as Pascal's point, can exist in any possible physical world, we might think (though this would make Pascal uneasy) he will exist. Consider: A die has six ways of coming down, for its possibility is the possibility of a six-sided entity. One can bet with certainty that at least one side will turn up, if the die exists and is thrown. Pascal would agree that at least one possible world exists, namely, ours. God, as a conceptually infinite being, has infinitely many ways of turning up. And his existence is compatible with any possible world. Given infinitely many chances, everything with a probability of greater than zero should occur. Does this suggest that God must exist?

Pascal would have been worried by any such argument. He would insist that we are, in saying these things, working in the world of the intellect even though we are trying to show how that world can be connected to the actual physical world. The physical world is in some way deficient with respect to its instantiation of the Platonic ideas. It is also deficient with respect to its ability to sustain the working out of moral ideas. Pascal's God must not be tied too closely to such a world. His coming is a gift.

To try to demonstrate the existence of God simply by reference to a doctrine of a priori probabilities would be to accept a view that was congenial to the neo-Platonic tradition in general, but not to Pascal or, for that matter, to Descartes: the doctrine that God and the created world in some sense *depend* on the same logical order—an order that might be thought to necessitate both God and the world. Pascal is very insistent that it is God, and not the logical order, who must be the source of everything. His reasons are no doubt partly theological, but they are also connected to his moral theory. He asserts that God cannot be the end to which everything ought to aim if he is not really the ultimate principle of everything.[45] One may detect here obvious stresses in Pascal's thought, which I address in chapter 5.

For now we should notice that the core of the problem about all our attempts to lay bare the ultimate rational order of things is that the human being is *"infini rien,"* a being who cannot be regarded as instantiating the real ideas and therefore cannot regard claims to knowledge with great confidence. It is from the observed physical properties of the die that we infer that it can, in fact, come down six different ways. Having decided that, we proceed easily to the arithmetic of the problem. But we do not have the opportunity to work with the infinity of God in this way. What is even more important, we do not have the opportunity to think of ourselves in this way. The human being has an infinite capacity to instantiate knowledge. He or she also has an infinite capacity to become the victim of illusion. Such a being does not have a neatly specifiable set of options like a six-sided die. The more we try to pin down human capacities, the more our "nothingness" will become apparent. Our intellect thrashes about trying to understand pale versions of real ideas. Our moral nature is feeble. When we look at our physical nature, we find only bits of matter that, in the past, composed other beings and will compose still other beings in the future.

Pascal makes clear very often that the concept of the infinite rightly belongs to our usable armory of ideas, and so we have something ultimate to hang on to. Yet the physical manifestations of the infinite are something else. So Pascal sometimes says that we ultimately know nothing at all about God.

Some element of experience is therefore surely desirable if we are to come to a reasonable conclusion about the issues at hand. In the physical order, we can rely only on probabilities. This is why we have to bet on the existence of God— if there is reason to think that we ought to believe in the existence of God. The intellectual order will not give us these reasons. In the intellectual order, we have some useful knowledge, but it is not clear how it is related to the other orders. Our only hope when we seek to know what we should do (or more dramatically, what we should *be*) is in moral knowledge.

Pascal, then, wants to tie some—to him—near certainties about the intellectual realm and the moral realm to a possibility about the physical realm, and this creates a situation in which it is reasonable to think that his bet is a good one in all the senses mentioned at the beginning of chapter 1. This seems an untidy way of doing things, requiring us to accept rather a lot and to bet on something that is far from a certainty.

To assess and to understand what Pascal is up to, I now outline the conceptual choices more clearly. To do this, I follow other attempts of the period to retain the basic elements of knowledge—our moral claims, our growing knowledge of nature, and the intimations that provoke us toward a natural theology with at least some rational elements. I follow some elements of Yves-Marie André and of Jean-Pierre de Crousaz and then return to the position of the skeptic to ask, finally, what is the best way to lay out the conceptual choices that are inherent in the situation that this historical study brings to light.

4

Human Dealings with God: The Development of the Neo-Platonist Responses

4.1 The Neo-Platonic Vision

THE NEO-PLATONIC WORLDVIEW CENTERS ON AN EASILY EXPRESSED DOCTRINE: The world is an ultimate unity understood as a series of emanations from God or the One. God, to make the world as he wants it must make some choices. He cannot create another God (that is logically impossible), and so he cannot instantiate the divine properties collectively. He must distribute them. Everything he creates will lack something. As the emanations descend from God, they have more and more imperfections. And so the confusion in our minds is understandably quite great.

The skeptic says that what our transactions with reason and nature suggest is that knowledge is not possible. We are too fallible. Our opportunities for error are too great. The world as we find it does not favor knowledge, and so the practice of believing is only an undesirable interruption in our lives. A neo-Platonist can answer that our confused world is just what *he* would expect, although such a philosopher must then explain how it is that this confusion does not finally impede knowledge.

If we begin, as Pascal evidently did, with the notion of a real infinity and accept it as a cornerstone of our knowledge of the intellectual order and *if* we can suppose that the intellectual realm contains the principles of all the orders, then the emanations become a reasonable hypothesis. The skeptic can react effectively only by denying that the notion of infinity intrudes on his scheme of universal doubt. Can the skeptic who does this doubt infinitely many things?

Pascal still insists that whether or not the God of Abraham and Isaac did manifest himself in *our* world, will do so again, and will save or damn us is a *betting* matter. This is because the gap between our concept of the infinite as an intellectual matter and the concept of the real infinite that *must* lie behind the appearances is too great for us.

One who wants to have a case against the skeptic and does not want to bet with Pascal must therefore find some way to bridge this gap. The answer traditionally lay in the notion that the world, to be fully intelligible, must be understood as, in the end, returning to the One. The science of Pascal's time did not encourage any such idea. Later philosophers use the idea of evolution as a way of reviving this traditional doctrine of the return,[1] but in the seventeenth century and generally in the succeeding century, scientists believed that nature was going nowhere. Indeed, it *could* not go anywhere. Its principles were given to it either eternally or by the act of a God who was not likely to change his mind.

Pascal himself thinks that in some way acting as if God exists—which includes believing in the existence of God—is a way of increasing the probability that he *will* manifest himself in our lives and, indeed, in our world.[2] That is what it is to bet on God's existence and ultimately why it is good.

But Pascal's Jansenist friends were always concerned lest we should think that we could save ourselves. For them, only the grace of God can save us. Thus, though Pascal speaks of our positive relation to God and of God's response to us, he reminds us that we are fallen creatures, prone to evil and error. Perhaps, even if we do bet on God's existence, it is, after all, only because God leads us to do so. Bets lie, if not within, at least on the edges of faith.

If one develops a full-bodied philosophy of the "return to the One" based on human activities and human possibilities, one can, perhaps, position belief in a more rational framework, but at the cost, no doubt, of accepting some human self-aggrandizement that may look like the sin of pride.

For Pascal, then, the difficulties in any neo-Platonist solution are evident. They either risk the sin of pride or they run counter to the claims of science. Indeed, the developing forms of neo-Platonism tend to do both. They explain the world in terms of an emanationist notion of causality that implies that much more is immanent in nature than science reveals, and they elevate the role of human creatures to what Jansenists think an intolerable level.

Inevitably after Pascal the latent unexplored possibilities came more clearly to the surface. We can most easily, therefore, understand the strength—or weakness—of Pascal's claims and understand why Pascal sensed that going too far along the neo-Platonist path would be disastrous by looking at what actually happened in the years immediately after Pascal proposed his wager. If the ideas he senses to be objectionable are latent in neo-Platonist positions more thorough-going than his, they should emerge as soon as thinkers begin to lay them out in detail. And so they do. I examine them to explain Pascal's point.

Malebranche searched for an acceptable solution within the confines of a mixture of Cartesianism and Platonism, the essence of which is that, in so far as we really grasp the principles in things, we think with God and "see all things in God." According to Malebranche, we ultimately share the ideas of God. Others were more doubtful. And even Malebranche required a complex line of argument to establish that what appears to us can really be an aspect of the divine mind.

Antoine Arnauld tries to stop this argument at the first move by denying that there are any real ideas, shared with God or not, that can link us to the Deity.[3] He argues long and sometimes ingeniously, but chiefly he supposed that Malebranche is unnecessarily multiplying entities by interposing "ideas" between things and us and that, in doing so, he only makes the problem of knowledge worse. Malebranche thinks that ideas *are* ultimately principles that can be manifested in different ways, and since principles can be shared, the linkage problem disappears. But Simon Foucher pursued Malebranche relentlessly, taking the view that we cannot move from our own ideas to any notions of external things. Even the certainties of reason (although he admits them) may apply only in our thought.[4] Malebranche's principles, in other words, may be grounded only in *us*.

Malebranche has perhaps even yet to be properly understood, but two of the early philosophers who tried to sort the problems out, the Swiss thinker Jean-Pierre de Crousaz and the French Jesuit Yves-Marie André, although largely forgotten, bring to light important possibilities, addressing above all the question of how our *activity* might both add to our knowledge and link us to God. Both, interestingly, were much concerned with aesthetics. I think they believed that the beautiful is something in whose manifestations we *do* obviously participate. I also think they hoped that if the beautiful could be linked to our activities and the good and the true could be linked to the beautiful, we would have a chance of working out some notion of our cooperation with God. André, partly because he was Malebranche's biographer, is better known,[5] although his treatise on metaphysics remains unpublished after 230 years. Crousaz's explorations of the ideas of the beautiful, the good, and the naturally fitting bear directly on our problem of knowledge and the return to God.[6]

4.2 Crousaz and Human Freedom

Jean-Pierre de Crousaz was born at Lausanne on 13 April 1663. He taught at Groëningen and in Switzerland and died in 1750. His work shows a constant neo-Platonism.[7] His most extensive study, *Examen du pyrrhonisme ancien et moderne,* a work of a million words, is in fact a sustained attack on Pierre Bayle, whose habit of slipping his skepticism into the notes and comments appended to the articles in his *Encyclopedia* struck Crousaz as both unfair and sneaky.

Although Crousaz gives an explanation of ancient skepticism that Marxists might now enjoy (he says it arose out of the need of honest men to question the claims of the Sophists who sold their knowledge as a commodity), its neo-Platonism is dominant. It often takes a curiously modern form. One is reminded of some post-Hegelians who thought of themselves as Platonists, especially Bernard Bosanquet.

Crousaz argues that moral knowledge arises out of the natural tendency of the human mind to realize its own nature in its knowledge of a complete and harmonious universe.[8] He argues that natural change can be understood only through the continuity of archetypal ideas whose possibilities are expressed through a gradually unfolding world.[9] In a related passage, he insists that "reason furnishes us with the ideas of perfection, equity, and justice" (which he says we ought to follow in interpreting the Scripture), and on the same page, he specifically acknowledges Plotinus.[10]

Indeed, without the variety of particulars, the real nature of the archetypes could never be known. Like Bosanquet's, Crousaz's position is always predicated on the search for a unity of explanation and of values. Thus, he has a chapter on the "beauty of virtue," and he argues that the foundations of morality and those of beauty are identical.[11] The argument is predicated on his five criteria of beauty: variety, unity, regularity, order, and proportion. A life that complied with those virtues, he says, would be bound to be virtuous as well as beautiful. Thus is beauty to be united under the form of the good.

Goodness and beauty (and by implication truth) are, therefore, open to human beings. This enables Crousaz to argue that we can play a role in the return to God, and he does so through an interesting theory of free will. This theory, expounded in various editions of his *Logique,* relies on neo-Platonic ideas, although in some later editions, he concentrates more clearly on a variant of the Cartesian position that free will is fundamentally a matter of immediate experience.

Unlike Descartes, however, Crousaz does not pinpoint the experience of reasoning as the essence of the matter, but wanders through a great variety of experiences. The argument to which I allude is expressed fairly clearly in the 1737 "*abrégé*" of his *Logique.*[12] In the 1720, 1725, and 1741 edition, he first argues that free will has to do with the future and not with the past.[13] He has already conceded that, once an act is performed, there is a sense in which it is a necessary act.[14] I think he means by this not only that the past cannot be changed but also that the act becomes integrated into a continuous pattern of explanation that extends over a region of time within which there is no special moment in which a change could have been made. But at the time that one chooses, the act does not yet exist and cannot, therefore, in another sense, be determined by the past unless some relation to the past can be established. The time in which one will act when one chooses to act is not yet here. One's acts, evidently, if they are free, originate in the present and need not be part of some continuous process that extends from the past through the present and into the future. Crousaz consistently attacks the presumption that because the past is determined, the present and future must also be—a presumption that, he says, makes what seems to be an intractable problem out of an ordinary situation that all of us understand as a matter of immediate experience. But he realizes that simply appealing to our immediate experiences of freedom would lead to indeterminism and not to any-thing like free will unless it were supplemented with some other explanation.

The explanation is that will determines itself through ideas that are not them-selves in time but can be expressed in time. The neo-Platonist theory of ideas thus becomes the basis of his argument. In his work on the human mind, he argues that the human mind is like God's mind in being in one aspect beyond time, but unlike God's mind in that it particularizes itself in its relations to the body. There are also Leibnizian overtones (despite Crousaz's repeated denuncia-tions of what he takes to be Leibnizian determinism),[15] for he argues the human mind is a monad or a substance that can be simply represented, but it becomes individuated through its bodily activities by giving unity to our innumerable perceptions.[16]

In the 1741 edition of the *Logique,* the freewill issue is posed as a question about how it is that God can know everything and yet it can still be true that human beings are free. The answer given in the Augustinian tradition is that God knows eternally while we know in time. This would tie in neatly with the view that we act at a moment, the present, which is not—and in one sense cannot be—determined by the past. The sense is that if the present is really unique in being a constituent of the real along with eternity, then ontologically it cannot be wholly determined by the past, for there must be some distinguishing element that makes it ontologically different from the past.

We can now put together the Crousazist picture of our situation. It turns out that we are in fact free and that our relation to God is that we express in time what he expresses in eternity. This explains the muddledness of our world and suggests a basis for our cooperation with God.

What does one say to the skeptic? One points out that the very nature of our freedom involves eternal ideas. The skeptic must claim freedom to believe or not. We should always remember in this context that what was thought most important in the skeptical position of the time is the claim that the skeptic is free, free to believe or not, free to believe what he or she wants. A possible answer to Arnauld's claim that we can do without "ideas" is that we need to have a relation beyond time in order to be free. If so, we are not multiplying entities beyond necessity when we introduce ideas. One could say to Simon Foucher (and others like him who attacked the Malebranchiste forms of neo-Platonism and who urged that we cannot escape the immediacies of our own thought) that the contact with eternity necessary to freedom surely leads us beyond our immediate selves. *If* we know we are free, then *we* know something about the world. And just this freedom is necessary to sustain Foucher's or any other skeptic's activities.

But these eternal ideas are intelligible only in terms of an eternal being. That is to say, eternal ideas that lead beyond the limits of the finitude of time lead to the notion of some being who is beyond that finitude. In the Augustinian world, the ultimate reals are the present and the eternal, and each takes its reality, although in different ways, from Platonic ideas in the mind of God. If the skeptic were to admit our contact with eternity as a necessary condition for intelligibility, the skeptical thesis would face shipwreck.

Our function in the world, based on this view, is to bring the ideas of God into the peculiarly human world that requires the exercise of freedom. God cares about us and our free actions, presumably, for just this reason. I think what Crousaz is hinting at, in defence of human intellectual and artistic life, is that believing in God consists in grasping the necessary ideas. Once one does this one sees, in the Platonist tradition, what it is that one ought to do—to act so as to bring the ideas effectively into the world of free human action.

4.3 André and Creativity

Yves-Marie André went further in insisting on the importance of creativity in man. André, a dozen years younger than Crousaz, was born at Châteaulin, Finistère on 22 June 1675. He died in Caen on 27 February 1764.[17]

He was Malebranche's biographer, and much more interested than Crousaz in the aspects of the arts that have to do with the production of genuine novelty. He was so interested in new forms that, 150 years afterwards, Jules Carlez, then professor of music at Caen, could write that André's work contained *"un flot d'hérésies."*[18] One of the things André noticed is that dissonance can have genuine merit in music.

André's most celebrated work, his *Essai sur le beau*, expresses his views on innovation, and while it concentrates on aesthetics, it provides a basis for a general value theory. To begin, there are certainly, he thought, essential ideas of the *"le beau"* given to us as innate or found by us through our association with the mind of God. These, no doubt, are what Crousaz was talking about.

André had to square his interest in creativity with what, even in 1744, was still his conviction that the truth lies in a Malebranchiste and Augustinian neo-Platonism. Both creativity and a dependence on a universal order of ideas, he says, are essential features of the human condition.

In his *Traité de l'homme selon les differentes merveilles*,[19] he underlines the dependence of human beings on a universal order of mind. He says in the *Discours sur la nature des idées* that it is worthwhile to notice that, from the point of view of philosophers, our knowledge of arithmetic, geometry, and morals is enough to show us how different are our ideas from our perceptions.[20]

Echoing Pascal, he urges that no one perceives the objects of which mathematics talks. He also speaks of the problem about infinities created by the fact that not only are the integers an infinite series, but also both the series of odd numbers and the series of even numbers consist of infinities that are equally long. How could we perceive such a thing? Such ideas must come from a mind quite different from anything associated with our perceptions.

Indeed, such infinities cannot be contained within our minds at all. They lead us on to God. Furthermore, André claims that no "social mind," no existent mind-in-common shared by two or more persons, could be made up solely of perceptions. Nor indeed, he thinks, would language be possible if it were simply made up of items of perception, for language, too, requires a common reality as well as access to structures that go beyond the finite. Just as numbers apply, in a sense, to everything, so do words.

This separation of perception and idea as well as the implicit (and often explicit) references to God are clearly Malebranchiste. Furthermore, André, like Malebranche, takes a firm stand against Descartes' view that God created all the ideas. God must have mathematical and other ideas before him to make a world, and André says so repeatedly.[21] The same view is expressed more clearly in his *Metaphysica.*[22]

But there is another issue that is not so clear. One might hold that God imprinted his divine ideas on our minds and that we are aware either of the imprint or of the divine ideas directly—that, as Malebranche said, "we see all things in God." Even if God did not create all the ideas, he could have imprinted any of them he wanted to on our minds. André is less clear about this, though I think that he would side with Descartes against Malebranche at least some of the time. One of André's Jesuit colleagues wrote him a letter of which André made a summary to send to Malebranche himself. The letter complained of André's complaisance in the face of "fanatical Malebranchistes."[23] The colleague says that Augustinian doctrine is sounder.

Augustinianism was taken to include the view that we sometimes obtain our ideas through secondary sources, even indeed, that God can and sometimes does imprint his ideas on things in the natural world from which we can abstract them. In his *Metaphysica,* André insists that God and his creatures have literally nothing in common.[24] What does happen is that the divine ideas give rise to ideas in our minds, and the ideas in our minds participate in their divine origins. But the ideas in our minds are really particulars. We use them to think and sometimes to think correctly. But they are not literally the principles that exist in God's mind.

When André speaks of ideas as if they were "innate," he means that these ideas reside in some mind or other to which we have access. So long as we have access to them, the effect of grasping ideas directly through the mind of God or indirectly through our own minds and even from natural objects would be much the same.

It is André's view that some "innate ideas" are necessary for aesthetics. We cannot explain our taste for proportion and for balance, for example, without recourse to ideas that are neither created by us nor empirical in origin. There are also *natural* ideas. They follow, that is, from our natures in the sense that they are formed in whole or part by our senses. Thus our senses have their own preferences and limitations. Excessively loud music is painful. Excessively soft music is beyond our reach, and as sound approaches these limits, it becomes irritating. The eye renders certain forms confusing and irritating—and so forth.

But there are also what Descartes called "factitious" ideas that we create. Bach used dissonances in his music, but André was one of the first to grasp fully the value of dissonance. Precisely by departing from what is expected either innately or by the senses, we draw attention to something new. And we can use these notions to make things aesthetically worthy. André's basic thesis in his *Essai sur le beau* is this: We know, if you like, that God exists because some ideas of the "beau" are at any rate deeply ingrained in our rational natures. In his *Metaphysica*, this argument is generalized so as to demonstrate the existence of God in terms of the immutability of all the most fundamental ideas that reason intuits (and so André attacks Descartes' view that God created those ideas and might have created them otherwise).

André, however, admits that the specific contents of our thought processes are mutable enough,[25] but through our grasp of the ideas of intelligence and perfection (ideas of which we see the necessity without fully assimilating them), we understand that there are immutable truths. In aesthetics, we are drawn to something not given to us by our senses and thus to something we cannot create and over which we have no influence. We also know that we are creatures, in important ways, of the structure of our own senses. Yet we are also creative, and it is in our nature to be so.

Indeed, André makes human openness fundamental to his metaphysics. Instead of the formula *"cogito ergo sum"* traditionally ascribed to Descartes, he insists that one should say *"cogito, existo, multa nescio."* Antoine Charma, his editor,[26] asked skeptically whether André could really believe that he had departed far from Descartes with this formula, but it seems to me clear enough that it *is* very different. What André is saying is that the very fact that I know I am a thinking being and also an existing being suggests that there is much that I do *not* know. This is true in principle because to be a thinking being is to be a free being and therefore to be in a sense an open being.

We should remember that Descartes himself made much of the connection between rationality and freedom and yet he did not derive this conclusion from it.[27] Thus, in his *Metaphysica,* André begins with the Cartesian question about my own existence and its nature as a thinking thing. And he accepts *part* of the Cartesian answer: I know that thinking goes on. But toward the end of this manuscript he insists that "I exist" does not follow from "thinking goes on," because that proposition does not give us knowledge of a truth that is a matter of known principle, but merely knowledge of a particular contingent fact.[28] "Thinking goes on" is something true in principle of any world in which *any* question can be raised. "I exist" requires an appeal to an inner sense that reveals an introspectable self.

The existence of thinking does follow from the fact of knowing. But even this is so, according to André, in a sense that explicitly depends on the presence of doubt rather than on a given certainty. André refers to Pyrrho by name, and he notes that it is certainly true that the Pyrrhonist can carry on doubting as much as he pleases, yet such a doubter may do so only at the cost of admitting that the doubting goes on.[29] But, then, says André, the Pyrrhonist really cannot withhold belief in the proposition that doubting goes on.

Moreover—and this is significant for the development of the argument—in the course of doubting, the skeptic is certainly aware that there is much to be known that he or she does not know. How else could doubt be said to arise? The distinction between the academic skeptic who doubts propositions and the Pyrrhonist who withholds belief is often blurred in the literature of the time, but here the Pyrrhonist is directly addressed. Such a skeptic says simply that all belief can be withheld—not that every proposition can be brought within the "sphere of the doubtful." But André says that, if one does withhold belief, one is still aware of some of the propositions from which one withholds belief. If one is aware of these propositions in a clear-headed way, one must know that there are many propositions that are *either* true or false. Hence, one knows that there is much that one does not know.

The effect of this argument is to situate the philosopher immediately as someone engaged in knowing, who nevertheless understands that he or she is a limited creature. Philosophers know that there is truth and that they do not have it. They know both that they are thinking beings and that they are finite ones. But they also know that there is truth.

Furthermore, this distinction between the knowing and doubting being and truth itself is a distinction that persists through all possible sequences of doubting. It leads to a kind of Platonism not properly recognized by Descartes. In his *Metaphysica,* André goes further in distinguishing himself from Descartes. For he denies that we actually know ourselves through ideas.[30] We know *"per ideam"* about truth and about doubt and that thinking is going on. But these are all occasions of knowledge of principle. And our own immediate existence is not a matter of principle. We actually know it, he says, by a direct inner sense, but this sense enables us to know things only because we can make use of ideas and *know* that we can. Our knowledge, that is, makes use of ideas, but there is an element of direct knowledge in which ideas play no part.

On at least one occasion André made his disagreement with Descartes and Malebranche explicit to his superiors. On 26 November 1712, he responded to his provincial, who had demanded that he should publicly renounce the philosophies of Descartes and Malebranche. André says that he combats these philosophers "in several places in my writings." He says he has disagreements "with M. Descartes in almost all of his metaphysics" and "with Père Malebranche" over "the manner in which he explains the free acts of the will."[31]

In one of his notebooks, now in the municipal library at Caen,[32] he has recorded an extract from Malebranche's *De la recherche de la vérité* in which Malebranche defines liberty, but here André has written *"verité!"*[33] I think the explanation is not that he was inconsistent or that he was trying to conceal the truth from his superiors. He agrees that liberty is the power to do what one wants to do, but he still disagrees with essential elements in Malebranche's account of free will.

In his *Metaphysica,* he works this out at length.[34] God, he says, is the author of all things, but he acts through the exemplary forms. Our world is divided in two. We meet approximations of God's ideas, not literally, but through things that participate in them. We do so in the physical world by encountering participating objects and in the mental world by encountering ideas of the sort Descartes describes: that is, particular states of mind that refer to the world. God's ideas are partially embedded both in physical things and in our ideas, and so the question becomes: In what sense can we be free? Is God not the author both of the physical world and of the mental world? André wants to divide the question; there is the issue of God's action in the physical world and that of God's action in the "inner world."

As for the physical world, it proceeds from the necessity of the exemplary ideas. André liked to say that the physical world proceeds altogether from the will of God. But his discussion of the nature of God makes it clear that the exemplary ideas are part of the essential nature of God and that God does not create them. God's volition is to act from his own nature—from the nature, that is, of the good itself. Action, for God, is the essential working out of the divine ideas. So such actions are the natural will of God, and there is no way we can interfere with them.

Yet this is only one way of looking at reality. There is another way that allows us to examine the situation from the point of view of our own inner lives. It is true that God has a real relation to every aspect of the world,[35] but we must understand that what this amounts to is that God has ideas of every element of the world and of every element as forming part of a perfected whole.

Nevertheless, this world also contains us, and we are beings endowed with free will. Because God has an idea of each of us as a free being, his idea of the working out of the world includes this idea of liberty. In the case of the physical world, whose objects proceed from their own natures, God's knowledge has a certain order; he knows how something will be prior to its being so in an absolute sense. Thus, André insists that it is impossible for anything really to interfere with our free will—"nothing can give the free act invincible pre-destination."[36] This is just because in the case of our inner life, the order of God's knowing is different.[37] He knows what we will do only by knowing how we will choose, and he must know our choice before knowing the outcome—for he has chosen to make us free creatures.

André is absolutely clear that we are free beings, but he also says that God's omniscience is not thereby limited. It is simply that God knows things in their necessary logical order. Logically, if we choose freely, we must do so before God can know what we have chosen. Furthermore, he says, there is yet another way of looking at the matter. We are rational creatures and the real acts of rational creatures—those actions that proceed from their real natures—are rational. But this rationality is part of the nature of God, and everything happens, in any case, as a result of "divine concurrence." One can say that our real actions, therefore, are the actions of God. Hence, in a way, "only God acts in us"[38]—but this is God expressing himself through us, and it in no way interferes with our own free will.

These are reasons enough for André's disagreements with Malebranche even though his admiration for him was always very great. For one thing, there is obviously much more to our active liberty than the power to reject specific courses of action, a power on which Malebranche insists above all. Malebranche concedes to the predestinarians that, in a general way, we are impelled toward the good by God but that we are free to reject particular courses of action. André, too, insists that we have negative powers, so that we can dissent from God, but we can also act positively and rationally, making, as it were, God's acts our acts and, in so doing, expressing our real natures.[39] Had Malebranche lived to read André's *Metaphysica,* he would have suspected that his biographer was lapsing into Spinozism.

There are also underlying issues. For André, the "way of ideas" (despite its failure to account for self-knowledge) takes precedence over both the preexisting presumptions of metaphysics and the preexisting presumptions of theology, and although there are strong marks of Cartesianism in his work, the neo-Platonic elements have become even stronger than they were in the work of Malebranche.

For Descartes, though God creates the world freely including even the laws of logic, the world is thereafter fixed by the trustworthiness of God. For André, everything, as he makes clear at the end of his *Metaphysica*, has a certain plasticity.[40] It does occur to André, as it would not occur to Descartes, that the whole world is subject to change as a result of its only partial participation in the divine ideas.

Similarly, it does occur to André, as it does not seem to occur *explicitly* to Descartes, that there is something very important to be added to the world by us. This last difference results from the fact that Descartes takes a different view of the *cogito.* He sees two main sorts of ideas: ideas of ourselves and of our inner lives and ideas of things external to us—either other people and God, or extended material objects. In orthodox Cartesianism, the analysis of these ideas reveals the distinction between primary and secondary qualities. Primary qualities belong to things. They are roughly those that, in modern terms, yield to the technology of measurement and so can be associated with extension. Secondary qualities are then seen to result from the interaction of these external objects and our minds. Although two kinds of ideas—those which do and those which do not vary with the state of mind and locale of the percipient—result, the necessary interaction is not impossible or surprising, for there are not two kinds of things but two kinds of ideas under analysis. It is true that, for Descartes, they are associated with two different quasi substances, but one must remember both that for him there is only one absolute substance and that the "kinds" of qualities are themselves qualities.

In principle, any substance could have any quality, so there is no problem about the interaction of substances. In fact, matter has only qualities associated with extension, and mind has only qualities that are not extended, but this is because God, the only absolute substance, has willed to keep the qualities separate. But the substances almost necessarily interact—for every substance would have every quality if it were not for God's will to the contrary. Thus Descartes thinks that God can make a single decision or a simultaneous set of decisions, and the result is a completed world.

For André, there is no way of imagining the world as completed except in so far as one is thinking of its perfected duplicate—the world of the idea of God in which God knows everything *sub specie aeternitatis*. For André, too, the *cogito* takes us only into the realm of principle that reveals at once our own limited being, which, just because it is limited, is open to change. To André, the whole world of partial participations is equally open to change.

André dictated a manuscript at Amiens, which is now lost and may have dealt in more detail with the questions posed here. But there is a section of his 26 November 1712 letter entitled *"Sur l'action des esprits, etc."*[41] In it, he suggests that Descartes and Malebranche alike forgot the dynamism of the human mind—that it is an activity, a power, and not merely something passive. It may be in and of itself a manifestation of the greater mind of God, but it is, nonetheless, active.

To make his scheme work, André continues to keep the distinction between two different senses of "idea." There are the ideas that are the exemplars through which God knows and creates the world (God knows and creates in a single act that André usually called the "divine volition"). These ideas give form to the things that participate in them and also give form to the contents of our minds but are imperfectly instantiated in the world and in the mind. Ideas in the second sense, the ideas in our minds, are psychological objects that participate in the divine exemplars but have a certain plasticity. The divine idea of liberty is also active in us and manifests itself both as a certain openness and (the other side of the same coin) a certain incompleteness in our affairs.

To explicate this better, I shall examine the Cartesian triformite analysis of ideas: there are ideas that are built into our minds, ideas that come from outside (and are caused by outside entities), and ideas that we create. The Cartesian account is open enough to allow for different versions of the ideas associated with God that Descartes calls innate. André, in his *Essai sur le beau*, uses this tripartite system and creates three categories of *"le beau"*—the essential *"beau,"* the natural *"beau,"* and the created *"beau."*

Descartes himself has various reasons for supposing that the idea of God is not adventitious or factitious. And many other reasons have been given for supposing that other ideas are in the same category. But all the claims commonly made on behalf of innate ideas have something in common. Such ideas have to do with the basic organizing structures of knowledge. Descartes' God is the author of the laws of logic. He provides the forms of all possible understanding. In a sense he is, if not reason itself, at least its source and its incarnation.

There is good enough reason to suppose that you cannot learn the most basic structures of organization—for to organize something presupposes either that you can recognize order in it or that you can impose some order on it. Even Locke's "empty cabinet" of the mind had to have some shelves in it. But for André, these "innate ideas" are those that show most directly the working of the divine exemplars. Thus such ideas tend to be active in and of themselves. Descartes associates this basic structure of the mind with the ideas that come directly from God and, once implanted, are fixed. It is thus really God who acts through innate ideas. This might seem to add to the glory of God. André certainly had no objection to the further glorification of God. But I think he suspected that the independence of humankind might thereby be obliterated as well.

Adventitious ideas would, I suppose, be admitted by anyone. There are forces outside us that cause us to have certain ideas, and we do not wholly control them. From André's point of view, however, there is more to the story. The Cartesian theory of adventitious ideas distinguishes between ideas of primary qualities and ideas of secondary qualities. Both are adventitious (or contain adventitious elements), but ideas of secondary qualities imply some reciprocal activity of the mind. It is not clear in Descartes (or sometimes even in Malebranche, as Simon Foucher never tired of pointing out) how the ideas in our minds can be known to be related to the things outside.

André has no trouble with this relation, because the divine exemplars inform the world and our minds alike. This is a very important point in the history of these disputes. According to André, the exemplars really comprise the nature of God. In so far as they are genuine ideas—and they cannot be otherwise—they cannot fail to be part of the knowledge of God. And what God knows exists. But God's knowledge of them is the knowledge that they *are* exemplary ideas. He understands them, that is, as leading naturally to their instantiations. Indeed, if

God creates according to his exemplary ideas they cannot fail to be instantiated. And every clear and distinct idea is a genuine idea. Therefore, in so far as we know that we have clear and distinct ideas, we know that we have ideas of the world.

Based on Descartes' view, this would not necessarily be true. According to him, no exemplars existed before God created the world. God creates them and could have chosen otherwise. Therefore, we might have clear and distinct ideas that inform no world, and this might be true even of adventitious ideas, for the world might imprint on us ideas God had not chosen to exist except *as* ideas in our minds.

Finally, what of factitious ideas? Are they simply assemblies of adventitious and innate ideas? Part of the difficulty with the Cartesian theory of clear and distinct ideas is that it suggests that elementary simple ideas cannot be misleading. Must not then all such ideas be considered in the same way? This is true, as we have just seen for André as well but with this difference: The divine exemplars are never perfectly instantiated in us, and therefore, there is always a critical analysis forthcoming of any claim to knowledge.

André was more seriously a partisan of Malebranche than of Descartes, and to one who follows Malebranche, the problem poses itself somewhat differently. First, André concedes that our own activity intrudes upon adventitious ideas so that, if you like, clarity is not enough.[42] André certainly agrees with some of his Jesuit critics that Descartes makes even God too arbitrary and does not allow enough power to ideas themselves. Adventitious ideas have, in some measure, their own way with us. Yet they take on particular forms in our minds and are particularized in a way partly given by their own natures and partly by the manner in which we deal with them.

Based on André's account, then, factitious ideas have an element of originality. They cannot all be analyzed into components from the outer world, but this does not wholly impede us in our search for knowledge. By relating ideas to their archetypes—as we relate perceived squares to the principles expressed through them when we do mathematics—we can combine the possibility of knowledge with the possibility of genuine creativity. The practical effect of this on André's thought is to create a triformite analysis of ideas in each domain. Just as the three kinds of ideas figure in art, so they figure in morals and in politics.

For André, the most general principles that relate all men and women are ideas central to human nature. These ideas come from God. Subordinate principles stem from the adventitious ideas that give us a sense of the kinds of creatures we are. Some things can be made good by the very choices we make, just as some things can be made aesthetically worthy by our activity. Some actions and some things we make are good because they are ours and express our own individuality, although such notions should not be exaggerated.

A theory such as André's seems to give a modest impetus to individualism; but it is carefully balanced. Innate ideas and ideas discovered in God alike bind us to the community of all humankind, for our innate ideas make us human. Adventitious ideas bind us to our nature as human animals; factitious ideas can give us our individuality. Once again, the theme is the unity of knowledge. All knowledge, whether in physics, morals, or aesthetics, is to be understood in terms of the three kinds of ideas. All human beings, if unified at base, are nonetheless individual, and to that extent, there is also individual knowledge. But in principle, all knowledge is bound together.

This theory explains how ideas latent in the debate might be developed and shows how one might construe a situation in which it is hardly necessary to bet as Pascal did. But it is unlikely to move the serious skeptic. I do not mean by the "serious skeptic" one who is simply looking for any clever sophism by which to evade serious thought but the skeptic who would like to have knowledge if it really could be had. Such a skeptic is likely to be made uneasy about the passage from the intellectual realm to the physical world of everyday events and about the way in which rather thin bridges are built between ideas we admittedly have and ideas that involve the existence of God.

Still, the argument does address some of Pascal's concerns. We can see how we can by free action come to have a legitimate place in the world and even how we might come to terms with God if he existed. In part, of course, it is exactly this that worries Pascal. In ceasing to be nothing, must the human being pretend to usurp the powers of the infinite? This is not merely the paranoia of a seventeenth-century man whose state of mind is in some way like that of a modern fundamentalist, although a depth psychologist might see the relation between the feelings of guilt that show themselves in Pascal's writings and the fear of placing too high an estimate on human capacities.[43]

The problem is, given that the human being is *"infini rien,"* how can such a creature come to have substantial being and how does this depend on the possibility that God might exist? André's solution does emphasize the need for creation, but does it not suggest that we already have a legitimate natural place in the universe? This position turns Pascal away from neo-Platonism. But in turning away, he must confront the skeptic, and I now turn to the question of how the skeptical position is to be conceptualized and how Pascal's wager might fit as one of the options open to the serious skeptic.

5

The Human Predicament and the New Skepticism

5.1 The Terms of the Skeptic's Trade

I ARGUE IN THE PRECEDING CHAPTER THAT IF WE TRACE THE LOGICAL UN-folding of the ideas that became central in Pascal's time, we can see just how crucial and problematic the understanding of the human condition and the human role in the universe became. Evidently, as he wrote the *Pensées*, Pascal was struggling to make sense of this situation, searching for a solution to the paradox that the human being is everything and nothing: *"infini rien."* What is not so obvious, perhaps, is that the educated thought of the time was changing the skeptical terms of trade in the intellectual marketplace. Pascal was suggesting that the position of the skeptic had been inverted.

Although the skeptic wanted to challenge all the things that other people claimed to know, there is a sense in which skepticism was never put forward as the doctrine that there is *no* knowledge at all. Skeptics offered grounds for their doubts or gave support for a policy of withholding belief. They always accorded doubting some measure of *preference* over believing, and reasons played a part in establishing that preference.

The "academic" skeptics, originally associated with the names of Arcesilaus[1] and Carneades[2] who took their stand on the Socratic claim that "All I know is that I know nothing," claimed to doubt all propositions expressing knowledge, at least all knowledge about the world. In some sense they had to know a great deal to know that all these propositions are doubtful. Those associated with Pyrrho of Elis held that what one should do is withhold belief.[3]

In either case, traditional skeptics doubted propositions about the external world but claimed *some* knowledge of their own inner lives. They thought they knew what they were recommending, and they thought they knew whether they were doubting or not. It is sometimes suggested that Pyrrho wanted to withhold belief on essentially moral grounds. That is, he thought that withholding belief is the better of two courses—the other being believing. He seems to have had in mind a calm life, although exactly what its other properties might be remains in doubt. His behavior suggests that he knew something about himself. Thus Cicero thought that Pyrrho was a skeptic about the external world, but not about moral matters.[4]

Certainly, whatever Pyrrho's own opinion, serious Pyrrhonists may want to reject not just moral knowledge but any claim to self-knowledge in the ordinary sense of that expression. But such thinkers will have to know whether or not they are doubting.

The strength of Descartes' response to the skeptics derives from the fact that they admit that they think about what they are and are not doing, especially about believing and doubting. If mere thinking (thinking about anything whatsoever) could establish anything about the world, the skeptic who took the traditional line would be trapped.

For Pascal, everyone can know about the "thinking machine," yet the human character itself, as opposed to the body, is not part of the subject matter of the sciences of the physical world. Furthermore, any serious inquiry into religious belief must suggest that believing itself is not a simple mental state. And such an inquiry is the essence of the *Pensées*.

To believe *seriously* in God is to *act* as if God exists. Pascal's whole attack on the Jesuits is predicated on the foolishness of muttering formulas and following rules. His view of his opponents is that they confuse formal observance with real commitment. Pascal thinks one must be committed to act as if one lives in a world in which God is real. I say more about how one Jesuit viewed moral commitment and about the issue of Pascal's attitude to "the world" later in this chapter and distinguish Pascal's view from that of Martin de Barcos. And I say more, too, about what it is to wager one's whole life on God. But it is the commitment to action, above all perhaps, that renders Descartes "useless" as a source of the grounds for serious belief in the existence of God.

5.2 The Human Condition

Seventeenth-century scientists had shown that, as knowing creatures, human beings can extend their minds to whatever the intellectual and the physical orders contain: *infini*. But when natural scientists and mathematicians came to address humanity, the person could no longer be found: *rien*. One might, like Bérulle, rejoice that Copernicus had turned the solar system inside out, casting earth out of the center and reminding us that the "sun of Plato" (the form of the good) is identified by Thomas Aquinas with the God of "our religion."[5] But Pascal's "thinking machine" had a worrying potential. Might it not someday be able to do whatever a human being can do in the physical world, even though Pascal believed that it contained not even one small thought?[6] Pascal believed that, from the perspective of the physical world, it is as if the intellectual world did not exist.

Physicists do not talk about thoughts. Therefore, in a sense, whatever can be done in the physical world can be done in a way that does not require thought in its description. The "thinking machine" shows that science is very likely to come up with a reasonably full account of the physical world, an account that reduces us to the matter-in-motion already suggested by Thomas Hobbes.[7]

Mathematics could reveal, Pascal thought, the true order of things, even though it is too profound for human beings to grasp.[8] If the mathematical and physical orders reveal everything, what is left of the human being? Such a being is nothing but a thinking reed.[9] Indeed, is not such a creature literally nothing? The ultimate sense is that there is nothing in the intellectual and physical orders *peculiarly* human, nothing to give us an essence of our own in the traditional sense.

There is, to be sure, the moral order. A. W. S. Baird repeatedly calls attention to Pascal's seeming uncertainty about natural morality.[10] One side of Pascal's ambivalent attitude toward natural morality depends, I believe, on the absence from his thought of a straightforward essence of humanity in the form of some property that might be found in the intellectual or physical world. In the Aristotelian tradition, natural morality depends on knowing one's essence and thus one's place in the whole order of things—for the essence of a thing distinguishes it from everything else and relates it, as well, to everything else. But there is another side. Pascal is not a proto-Sartrean who thinks that humanity has nothing natural on which to depend for some guidance. For our being, whatever it is, extends to all the orders, and as Baird suggests, there is a hierarchy of values implicit in the orders. Human beings are somehow to rise above the mere physical order. Because our being has more than one dimension—we live at least in the intellectual (which includes the mathematical) order as well as in the physical order—we have choices to make, and having choices to make, we have a moral dimension. But how are we to make our choices?

There is an "infinite distance" between the orders—intellectual, physical, and moral—at least in the sense that whatever is in one simply does not appear at all in the others. There is thus an implication that there must be a fourth order—an order of orders.[11] The first clue, perhaps, is that humanity is to be seen as a very special kind of connecting link.

"What is man in nature? Nothing in relation to the infinite, everything in relation to nothing—a location between nothing and everything."[12] If we look for human beings in any one of the orders, we shall not find them. They are neither physical objects nor Platonic ideas. Their milieu is certainly in the order of charity, the moral order, but it would be absurd to say that a human being is an act of charity (even an expression of God's charity). Rather such a being is the medium through which such acts are expressed, just as charity itself requires a just measure of feeling and reason. There are moral principles, but merely acting on the rules produces the kind of emptiness of which Pascal accuses the Jesuits.

There are moral feelings ("the heart has its reasons"[13]), but to act on mere feeling is to act as an animal—something justified in animals but not in human beings.[14]

Human beings must keep the balance. The "nothingness" that is humanity *in nature* is often *rien*, as in the *"infini rien"* at the beginning of the wager fragment.[15] The origin of *rien* is in the Latin *res,* so that what is *rien* is whatever is not a thing. *Néant* is derived from the scholastic Latin *non ens,*[16] literally "non being." *Rien* occurs 188 times in the *Pensées*, against 25 occurrences of *néant*. *Néant* is frequently used in religious contexts. A significant occurrence of *néant* in a passage having to do with humanity and nature, however, is in the long fragment about science and the human being in nature, in which humanity is said to be *néant* in the face of all and everything. But much of this fragment concerns the human creature's being in relation to God, and the point there is that the human person does not, in Pascal's view, have being of its own but rather reflects or expresses the being of God in a neo-Platonic way.[17] In fact all of the occurrences of *néant* are in a few fragments. They mainly divide between instances associating *néant* with the "trembling" of humanity before God and the infinite and instances stressing the contrast between human nonbeing and the being of the deity.[18] But Pascal uses *rien* to designate the "nothing" in the "all or nothing" between which the human person is a mean.[19]

The message appears to be that the human person is not a thing in the world. We have a different sort of being. But the being that we can express is not, therefore, something that derives from a condition of the world. It must come from somewhere else. The contrast between humanity and God is not the same as the contrast between humanity and things. Our greatness is our capacity to express everything—that is, to be the vehicle through which God could manifest himself if he chose.[20]

Certainly, humanity is nothing *and everything* in the sense that we contain the whole of reality within our potential knowledge. The skeptic, if you like, can turn the world inside out and insist that what we know is all within us and, hence, that in the physical world to which the sciences reduce us, human beings are themselves only creatures of our own mind. Simon Foucher and Bishop Berkeley (in related but very different ways) argue just this, and Leibniz argues it in a third (and essentially unrelated) way.

But let us look, for a moment, at the skepticism that goes with the traditional view that some element or elements of the human inner life are intrinsically more certain than knowledge of the external world. François de la Mothe le Vayer, something of a Montaigne imitator, tutor to a prince, and a confidant and functionary for Cardinal Richelieu, is an example of this type of skeptic.

There is still some dispute—a lot of honest uncertainty—about just how La Mothe le Vayer saw himself. There is still doubt about whether, for instance, he really took his religion seriously. It has even been suggested that he and Pascal held much the same kinds of views.[21] This seems to me a serious misunder-standing, not because, as Charles Chesneau argues, it is uncertain whether La Mothe le Vayer's religious beliefs were serious or not,[22] but because Pascal precisely does not hope to trade off doubts about the external world against some inner certainty (his ability to know whether he believes or doubts) as La Mothe le Vayer frequently does.

I think, though, that we can make a kind of sense of La Mothe le Vayer's overall position. He certainly put forth a very clear fideist position in a small work on the immortality of the soul in which he specifically argues (as many had before him) that this question cannot be definitively settled by reason.[23] Yet he sometimes allows reason considerable say in religious matters. His treatise on the salvation of the pagans[24] aroused the ire of those who thought he was far too soft on them. He held that reason allows them a place Christianity seems to deny them. An attempt to form a balanced picture of La Mothe le Vayer suggests that, with his love of classical learning, his frequent respect for traditional kinds of reasoning, and his skepticism about knowledge of the external world, he was a romantic classicist fighting a rearguard battle against modern science.[25]

He was rooted in his faith chiefly because he was a traditionalist. The faith was part of a tradition that buttressed the social order. He thus had claims to be a genuine believer even though his belief was of a kind against which Jansenists and Pascalians naturally protested.

La Mothe le Vayer was a man hankering for a fast-vanishing age when the human condition was still much as it had been in late classical antiquity. If he has any intellectual certainties, they are historians' and lawyers' certainties such as he reveals in his historical writings and in his treatise on "proof by comparisons of writing," which deals with problems posed by standards of proof in the criminal and civil law and their relation to written documents—problems that, he says, came up all the time at the palace (where he consulted with Richelieu).[26] He could toy with the idea that if skepticism is true, all propositions are equally good, and one can choose whichever of them one likes. He could make an exception to his skepticism for the classical learning he loved (and even for the pagans, including Confucius, he admired and hoped were saved), but this is because the figures of classical antiquity, including his beloved pagan thinkers, lived on as characters in a kind of historical story. The standards for such stories interested him a good deal, and he wrote much about history.[27] He was concerned to emphasize documentary authenticity and to emphasize the qualities necessary for the historian, essentially open-mindedness (the ability to take all points of view) and great learning. History lies within books and papers and brings out human qualities that most approach the divine.[28]

Pascal lived in a different world, and he knew it.

It is true that at first sight the remarks on skepticism in the *Pensées* may appear confusing, but I think they all make sense once one has seen them together in the context of Pascal's thought and in the main currents of the time. Pascal mentions skeptics of one sort or another in twenty-three *pensées*. Twice Pascal also speaks of *libertinage*.[29] All but two of the twenty-five mentions of various sorts of skepticism seem to fit into one of two patterns. The first approaches skepticism as a kind of direct trade-off. The skeptic argues about what is to be believed and what is doubtful and about what can be doubted in the face of what one believes. The certain is certain in contrast to some doubt, and the doubtful is doubtful in contrast to some certainty. The second pattern discernible in Pascal's discussions of skepticism in the *Pensées* involves an indirect trade-off. It takes the form of a Platonic search for something that, like justice, seems a doubtful element in knowledge because none of the proffered accounts seem acceptable. But their unacceptability is relative to some hidden standard. It is only as the debate wears on in Plato's *Republic* that we discover why we do not like the definitions of justice proffered early on.

The most important example of Pascal's first pattern is a long discussion, which has the numbers 246 and 131 respectively in Lafuma's Delmas and Luxembourg orderings, in which Pascal sums up the case for and against skepticism.[30] Understanding this passage is not easy. It begins with the claim that the skeptic can argue that, without faith and revelation, we have no certainty about *"ces principes."* What *"these* principles" are is obscure. Here we are in trouble because of the fragmentary nature of the text, but in the Delmas and Luxembourg ordering, it appears with others having to do with human nature and experience. Brunschvicg finds similar companions for it. Chevalier locates it together with questions about religious belief that raise the same point.[31] Indeed, "these principles" seem, from what follows, to have to do with what we know about ourselves and our origins. Pascal goes on to borrow from Descartes and to say that, apart from faith, we have no means of knowing if humanity was created by a malign demon or not. Finally, we do not even have any certain means of knowing if we are awake or asleep. Thus our *lack* of self-knowledge—our knowledge of our natures and our origins—puts the skeptic in a strong position. The terms on which the skeptic could sell ideas have truly changed. I argue below that this is not merely a matter of the surface effect of the currents of modern thought, but that the underlying issues emerge clearly when one examines what happens when the skeptic offers a serious challenge to the acceptance of these terms.

That it is right to interpret *"ces principes"* in terms of the importance of understanding that what we know of the world has left us with a problem of self-knowledge but not, in the same way, with a problem about our knowledge of the world is confirmed by Pascal's arguments *against* the skeptics, which follows immediately in this summary of the skeptical situation. He says that "we cannot deny natural principles if we speak in good faith and sincerity." "Natural principles" in this case are principles of external nature, as opposed, apparently, to the principles of our own nature (which have a religious origin). "Good faith and sincerity" may have various meanings, but Pascal has in mind, I think, beliefs on which one is prepared to act. In Pascal's time no one could in good faith and sincerity seriously doubt that those who traveled constantly west across the oceans must eventually return to their points of origin unless they could not find their way across Panama or they encountered physical obstacles later on. In Pascal's time the roundness of the world was a fact; the creation of empires made feasible by shipbuilding techniques and celestial navigation was another fact. The growth of great cities that necessitated Pascal's bus system (so that the poor could work outside their own *quartiers*) was related to these facts. Even the "thinking machine" had to be accepted along with its intended use: It was created to help Pascal's father, who was a tax collector, and anyone who thought about it would have realized what it could do for (and to) the world.

Being *sincerely* skeptical about the external world was becoming harder, even as being sincerely skeptical about the inner life was becoming easier. Thus in the same fragment, Pascal says, "What a chimera is man, what a novelty, what a monster," and he adds darkly, "Man is beyond the powers of man."

The fact is that, as Pascal insists, "Nature confounds the skeptics and reason confounds the dogmatists." *One* sense of this statement is that we have, after all, a natural propensity to believe. Our nature as animals who act in the world gives us a kind of animal faith that makes disbelief difficult. But it is equally true that the claims nature apparently authorizes were becoming more and more impressive. Admittedly, reason continues to confound the dogmatists in the sense that what cannot be sincerely doubted and what can be proved are two different things. The two might coincide, in Pascal's view, in mathematics, for which there are proofs. But in mathematics the ability to entertain sincere doubt is large because there is a misfit between the profound order revealed in mathematics and the things the human mind has a propensity to believe.[32]

Even in intellectual matters, the Pyrrhonists did not strive to obtain the mean Pascal recommended,[33] and so he says that "obstinate" (or "opinionated") is the right epithet for them.[34] One ought rather to doubt where reason is inconclusive, assure oneself where one can, and submit where one must.[35] The reference to submission suggests faith. But faith enters in a curious way that involves a major underlying theme in an argument with the skeptics.

In the passage in which he speaks of the skeptic Arcesilaus (who was said to have become a dogmatist), Pascal says that he, Pascal, had long believed in justice and was right to do so, although he did not really know what justice was until he discovered what God intended to reveal.[36] Thus, although he doubted and changed his mind, he says that he really kept his old opinion: there *is* justice.

Arcesilaus was an academic skeptic, the sort addressed in Augustine's *Contra Academicos.*[37] The more Arcesilaus doubted, the more dogmatic he became in Augustine's view, for it was Augustine's view that the skeptic becomes a dogmatist because he knows that every proposition is doubtful. Pascal is gently mocking himself for being like Arcesilaus, but there is a serious undertone.

If one listens to the undertone, one discerns a significant pattern in Pascal's thought. The problem about justice (in part at any rate) is this: One who doubts any particular claim about what justice is does so because he thinks that the definition offered—say that justice consists in giving like to like, or giving each their due, or doing what is best for the least advantaged, or whatever—is inadequate. One may not know what justice is, but one supposes that there is something better than what is offered in the definition one is given. Usually the reason is (as in Plato's *Republic)* that when justice is introduced as a topic, the definition allows us to confuse justice (or *whatever* is to be defined) with something else we know to be different. The skeptic is also, although in a different sense, a believer.

The case of justice is instructive. Justice for human beings would seem to consist in what is appropriate to each nature. But, to repeat, humanity has, in Pascal's view, no nature, as such. We are *"infini rien."* In so far as we are *"infini"* it must be God—the infinite being—who is expressed through us. The more one is skeptical about human justice, the more one sees that justice is divine. Indeed, Pascal says specifically that human justice is not just[38] and that the ultimate (but necessary) ignominy of Jesus was to be condemned to death by the "forms of justice."[39] It does follow that, since human beings are equal, they ought to be treated equally. Pascal even extends this to equality in the possession of goods,[40] but he thinks that people cannot tolerate an equality such as this and, instead, have to justify force to get their way.

Through these fragments the argument thread goes something like this: Human beings cannot grasp justice for themselves because they derive their natures from a being whom they do not grasp or else because human nature is nonexistent or of the wrong kind to be a source of justice. But our skepticism about the claims of human justice nonetheless leads us to suppose that something better fits justice than any definition humans can arrive at. If justice must be better than human beings can contrive, it must come from something better than human. It must come from the source of our being. Hence, like Augustine's academic skeptic, Pascal becomes a dogmatist—and he mocks himself.

One would think that there is an obvious line of escape by simply doubting that there is such a thing as justice at all. But a Pascalian cannot do this because, for him, there *is* something relevant one *does* know. One knows that humanity extends across the three orders and that there must be some way for us to reunify ourselves. We surely have bodies. We surely do mathematics. And we must make moral choices. We can attain the repose that Pyrrho sought only by finding a just balance among the various orders.

If we have a ground for being skeptics based on this account, it is that the human person is an entity who must thrive in all three orders but who has no real being—no being properly human—in any of them and thus cannot seem to find a place in the universe. And if justice is even possible, there has to be a way of fulfilling its demands.

Plato thought that the just society must be a society in which each of the aspects of the human soul has a place. A Pascalian must suppose that, if justice can be attained by human beings and human societies, it must involve a just proportion between the three orders. The classical notion of justice was not infrequently taken to involve the idea of human nature and human society as a reflection of just proportions of the cosmos. But if one takes the more ordinary modern view that justice involves chiefly moral, social, and political relations among individuals, the problem will continue to arise for a Pascalian. A just society is one in which good can be perceived to be good by its participants and so does not need to rely upon the "might which cannot be forced to obey justice."[41] This intelligible right ordering requires that the needs of the body be taken care of (hence Pascal's recognition of the justice of equal distribution of goods). But the needs of the mind and the needs of the moral order must also be addressed.

We may mock ourselves for not being skeptical enough, but still, we are forced by physical nature and by our own natures into a position in which we have to contemplate justice and in which natural reason reveals some of its nature although not all of it. In being so forced, we must consider God, the being through whom we find our reality.

Justice is only one exemplary case. Our conviction that there is a truth also gives us ground for doubt, and in so far as this is its logical function, we must hold that there *is* truth. This seems to contradict the thesis that we have "an image of truth" but "possess only lies." But Pascal *does* insist that "we have an idea of truth invincible to all Pyrrhonism."[42] The explanation is that, as far as we can make out in the here and now, everything we can understand is true in part and false in part, and "nothing is purely true." But this is not to deny that we have an idea of truth in the different sense in which a Platonist has an "idea of justice," which cannot at present be adequately explicated but which enables such a philosopher to play a part in a Platonic dialogue just because it engenders the sense that there is something wrong with the various definitions offered.[43]

Such considerations may tell us why we go on searching for the correct explication of our idea of God, but they do not give us any actual information about God. Once again we seem to be in a trap. We cannot quite escape the notion of God, but we have no adequate natural knowledge of him, either. This is why Pascal, directing the searcher after God to seek out both the believers and the skeptics, remarks that the searcher will be filled with misgiving.[44]

Thus, "Pyrrhonism is true" in a certain sense. Nature reveals the need for God and for justice but does not give us enough information to sustain proper religious beliefs. Before Jesus, when, according to Pascal, human beings had only nature (and perhaps inadequate revelation) to rely on, they got their religion wrong.[45] Thus, too, Pyrrhonism does feed our religious beliefs.[46] If we did not doubt human capacities, we would not see the need for religious belief.

Finally, Pascal says that not grasping the different possibilities of humanity— our greatness and our limits—is the source of the different schools of philosophy: "Stoicism, epicureanism, dogmatism, [skeptical] academic philosophy."[47]

So far so good. But the first of two really difficult passages is one in which Pascal says, "All their principles are true, those of the Pyrrhonists, of the Stoics, those of the atheists. But their conclusions are false because the opposed principles are true also."[48] "They" presumably are philosophers of various sorts. The problem is to determine what "their principles" are about. It does not seem that Pascal could mean that the substantive principles of these thinkers are true, for they obviously contradict one another. What seems to be intended are methodological principles. And this makes sense in the context. Each philosophical school Pascal mentions is noted for some methodology. The skeptics apply doubts or withhold beliefs wherever possible. The Stoics are noted for their logic and for their tendency to order the data so as to exhibit universal laws. It is not so clear who the atheists with a methodology might be—chiefly, perhaps, the people suspected of pantheism, such as Bruno and Spinoza, who are noted for trying to mould all the data into unified wholes.

Pascal would have accepted each of these methodologies in its proper place. The problem the passage suggests is just that the conclusions clash because these philosophers ignore the methodologies of the others. What happens if one combines them? Some measure of confusion must result, but Pascal is not averse to the confusion.

The problem of confusion brings us to the second difficult passage. In it Pascal says that he treats his subject with too much honor to impose an order on it because he wants to show that there is a sense in which the subject is really incapable of order.[49] The passage begins with the word *"Pyrrhonisme."* It goes on, "I will write, here, my thoughts without order and not perhaps in a confusion without design. That is the real order, one which always marks my order with disorder." The point, in part no doubt, is that the actual order of thought is not the polished order later imposed on it. It may be that the real order of thought reveals a more profound order in its surface disorder. But I think that, as is often the case in the *Pensées*, although the surface meaning is also intended, Pascal intends more. The truth is that there is and must be a certain disorder to the world itself unless it is recovered by God, "saved," if a world can be saved, or returned to the One as the Neoplatonic tradition has it.

Therefore, real thought, here and now, about the human condition must be marked by a certain disorder within which the real order can be found. Ultimately, the confusion is not absolute, however. Once we see what the situation is, we see that we must make a wager. Pascal insists that there are not many true Christians. Many believe through superstition, and nothing justifies that. By contrast, *"libertinage"* prevents others from believing. *Libertinage* here seems to mean "sheer willfulness." Not many believe on the right grounds.[50] But what this means is that, faced with many uncertainties, plagued by superstitions, corrupted by the human will, we still can know that we must make a choice even though the choice is no more than a wager.

5.3 And Now to Bet

The whole argument is supposed to tend toward the view that one should bet on the existence of God—that is, that one has enough information to make this a good bet and not enough information to be certain.

Although Pascal is right to believe that the prospect of an infinite return on one's investment justifies, at least technically, any risk whatsoever, the gambler nonetheless needs a good deal of information. Here we need to remind ourselves of the salient issues. One who bets has to know fairly clearly what he or she is betting on and how to construe the betting situation. Are there other bets with similar payoffs? Of what exactly does the supposed infinite payoff consist? How does one choose among infinite payoffs? (Remember that, because Pascal himself has told us that infinity plus one is the same number as infinity, an infinity of mild pleasures might add up to the same amount of pleasure as an infinity of bliss.)

But it is not so much these quasi-technical issues that puzzle us. The central question is about how to conceptualize the choices facing a human being. Pascal's thesis, evidently, is that if the human person is nothing in itself and everything potentially then we must, if we can find out how to do so, act so as to increase our chances of escaping nothingness. We must actualize our infinity if we can by making all being part of our own nature.

The point that I have been inching toward since the beginning of this chapter is that the "nothing" that concerns us as human beings and with which we are inevitably involved has, in itself, come to our attention because the notion of the self as a continuing, distinct substance that can be clearly known has faded. The coming of modern science has left us knowing much about the world and little about ourselves. The problem is not merely that psychology is not as well developed as physics; the problem is more that the self cannot even easily be found in the world. Even psychology tells us more about behavior than about the traditional "psyche."

The lost self cannot be recaptured by studying physics or behaviorist psychology. It also cannot be recaptured by reading Descartes (learning about the intellectual world) or, per se, by the study of morality. Human beings can show themselves in their potential as the manifestation of the infinite only by doing something in the world.

Pascal's recommendation is that what we ought to do is believe in God. But believing in God, as he says, is behaving in a certain way—that is, behaving as God would expect us to behave if he did exist. To do this in turn is to treat everyone as if he or she were saved.

I argue that Pascal would insist that the bet must be a good one in three different senses: it must be justified by whatever we know; it must be morally good; and it must, like any other bet, be likely enough to succeed to justify the odds. (Even with an infinite payoff, it must have some positive chance of success, however small.)

Whether Pascal's wager *is* a good bet depends, ultimately, on two different sorts of considerations. One concerns the question of whether or not the framework in which it arises has been correctly described—whether or not the human predicament is or is not as Pascal says it is. If that question is answered in the affirmative, the second kind of consideration concerns the options open to us.

By itself the question of the intellectual terms of trade—the question of what certainties the skeptic at any given moment feels are acceptable as a condition for the doubts he wants to press—is inconclusive and might, indeed, involve no more than the superficialities imposed on us by the temper of the times. The culture of classical antiquity made certain assumptions about the inner life seem natural. Pascal's culture (like ours) makes scientific claims seem powerful. I argue that Pascal's case has deeper roots. But it is true the outlook for a skeptic hoping to attract others to his way of thinking had been changed by Pascal's time decisively and in a way that proved lasting. Even if one could still be content with the position of La Mothe le Vayer in 1650, Pascal rightly discerned that it was becoming more difficult each year. Pascal suggests that nature—"nature" considered as the universe at large and our own "natures" in relation to one another—seems to conspire to create a belief in the reality of the world as the natural sciences describe it. In 1650 it was *possible* to doubt the whole body of conclusions ascribed to science, but it was difficult. It was possible, too, to doubt that the methodologies used in the various sciences, whether taken singly or collectively, were in any way likely to be adequate to the disclosure of the nature of reality. Later there would be profound attempts, the seeds of which perhaps are in the work of La Mothe le Vayer, to vindicate the claims of historians that their knowledge was more reliable than that produced by the scientists. But in

Pascal's time, one could see the success of science changing the world around one, and the pressure to believe was already very strong. By contrast, it was all too easy to fail to find the human self in the world described by the sciences. Our world is very different, but the path from Pascal's "thinking machine" to our own technology is too easy for us not to notice that Pascal had discerned a changing pattern in the skeptical terms of trade—a pattern that would subsequently only grow more obvious.

It is very important to notice, while we are trying to get Pascal's project straight, just what the best prospects would be for a serious skeptic and just how taking advantage of those prospects would affect Pascal's project. Suppose one pursues to its logical conclusion the project begun by Cardinal Newman in his *Essay in Aid of a Grammar of Assent*.[51] Newman there argues that logic can never compel any belief; we can question any proposition and any argument. Whatever the standard for accepting a proposition or accepting the validity of an argument, we can ask for more evidence. We can always ask for new premises. We can even ask for a new logic. But consider the conclusion that Newman seems to aim at: If it is really true that we can question any belief (at least logically), then it follows that we are free beings who can choose. The progeny of Pascal's "thinking machine" are the computers we confront in our daily lives. Invariably they have to accept some proposition or other. If they reject every proposition, they are simply not working. *If* there is no proposition that we cannot reject, we are not programmed *in the way that these computers are programmed* or in the way that Pascal's "thinking machine" and subsequent discrete state machines are programmed.[52]

Because human beings are not composed of "discrete states" and cannot be found in the computable, scientific world, Pascal regards the human person as *rien*. Yet he could argue that we are both nothing and free. The paradox of nothingness and freedom dissolves only if we act. It is only when we choose to act that we become something. We must act in order to be anything at all. If we must act in these conditions of free uncertainty, we must bet.

The soundest bets must go with the best knowledge. Still, what Pascal is suggesting is that our best knowledge is not some collection of scientific facts, but the knowledge that we can extend the human mind to indefinitely many subject matters. This is partly a matter of experience, but it is also partly a matter of mathematics, which, as Pascal says, sustains us in our belief in infinity. Pascal is a little uneasy about the "thinking machine," but he thinks he can understand its principles and the limitations they provide: this is reasonable.[53]

Pascal is being reasonable, therefore, in urging that we should bet on our infinite capacity. If we do have an infinite capacity, then no finite knowledge accounts for everything. The contents of all the physics books cannot account for all that there is. Pascal says we sense that there are other realms. Those who followed him in the line of thought that is peculiarly his, the line that builds most heavily on our grasp of the mathematical infinity, have often agreed. In our own time, Georg Cantor and Kurt Gödel revealed themselves as "mathematical mystics."

When Pascal says, "nature confounds the skeptics," we can easily understand at least part of what he has in mind, but we need to remind ourselves of the complex twists that the idea of nature takes. Pascal intends both to remind us that we are believing animals and that scientific claims to knowledge are difficult to resist. Here we see the intellectual and the physical orders at work. But we are creatures who also have, in Pascal's view, a place in the moral order. Thus the idea of the "natural" world as a moral order is understandable. Pascal would not have been surprised to find people in our time who credit "nature" or their own "natures" with encouraging them to set limits on technology that might otherwise dominate the environment. But he would have thought that such people are not literally acting on some knowledge not available to their opponents but are making what they think is the best bet on the future, thereby establishing their own presence in the world in a special way.

In various senses, then, people not infrequently feel that they must bet or act in a way that constitutes a bet in order to *be*. On the face of it, a bet that we have infinite capacities and a place in the three orders seems quite plausible. But this plausibility depends on what one thinks of the actual options. Pascal often talks as if the choice were between betting on the Christian God and leaving oneself as *rien*.

Yet it is not clear, even from Pascal's own showing, just how the Christian God fits into the picture. We need to do two things: one is to put a little more precision on Pascal's notion of God; the other is to relate this notion to what we have already seen as obviously competing notions. Only then can we see to what extent other options are reasonable.

Pascal does speak of the "God of Abraham and Isaac," but Jesus is mentioned some fifty-five times in twenty-four *Pensées*. The emphasis is always on Jesus as a figure who appears in *this* world—on his humility, his simplicity of speech, his origins, his generosity to us, and on the need to approach him without pride. The God on whom we are to bet is, indeed, the God of the Incarnation.[54] The larger questions about the eternal economy of the Trinity do not seem to play an important role in the *Pensées*.

From the point of view of someone who wants to understand the wager, however, perhaps the most revealing text is the one in which Pascal insists that Jesus is to be found in each of us.[55] For this is precisely the issue: If we are to instantiate the infinite, then God must be expressed through us. This above all animates Pascal's bet. It gives us a claim to *a chance* at being "saved"—for to be the expression of the infinite and eternal is to play a part in the history of the infinite and eternal, which would amount to one's justification. The idea of the infinite and its need for expression gives intellectual sense to the wager, and this idea of God being expressed through all of us and the need to act as if everyone were saved gives moral justification for the wager proposal.

Pascal spells this out in some detail; the presence and nature of Jesus is expressed through "all that is great" in any of us. In order to do this, God must assume in his mortal life as Jesus the form of "all that is poor and abject," for otherwise he could not be "present in all persons"[56] and also "the model for all conditions of men." He appears in rich and poor and in kings as well as in the humblest of people, but apparently only the good qualities of human beings represent the person of Jesus.

The implication, here and elsewhere, is that Jesus appears through *particulars,* which presents a difficulty. From principles one can make inferences, but particulars have no necessary connections to one another. Pascal seems to admit this and to draw an unhappy conclusion from it. Can we infer, indeed, that God will really save anyone? In response to such questions, Pascal says, "My God! What a way to talk! Would God make the world in order to damn it? Pyrrhonism is the cure . . . for this vanity!"[57]

There are clearly two difficulties here for one who wants to wager. One concerns what we know about God's future behavior, the other what we know about our own future states. If I bet on a chariot race, I make certain suppositions about how the horses will run based on their past performances, the record of the driver, the frequency of spills, and so forth. But Pascal does not think we have or should demand this kind of information about God. There is a chance that God is reliable. He does have, Pascal thinks, a moral duty not to lead us astray.[58] But we do not know enough about his motives to know whether he shares our goals or not, and we really do not know who is saved and who is damned.

Furthermore, in two different senses, Pascal thinks we ought to bet our lives on the proposition that God exists. One is that believing in God consists in acting in a certain way that orders one's whole life. It is not as if God is relevant only to part of our lives. The other is that the wager implies that making the wrong bet or making no bet at all increases the actual risk of damnation, a prospect that Pascal sees as an infinite loss. One can argue—and Pascal does argue—that what economists would now call the incremental cost of betting on God is not very high. One ought to behave well anyhow, and believing in God consists chiefly in behaving well. The central ingredient is losing one's self-centeredness. One shows one has done this by treating all others as if they were saved.[59] Thus what one needs to do in addition to what one ought to do anyway is slight.

If I bet on a race, I also think I know something about my own future states, that the payoff will be useful to me or to others that I want to help. The implication of much that Pascal says, especially when he brings the prospect of damnation into the argument, bears on a future life, and indeed, he stresses that immortality is among the most important of questions.[60] Yet our existence is inherently precarious. We sit uneasily between nothing and infinity. Pascal does not in fact offer us very much to place in the context of the debates about immortality that have characterized Western philosophy. He is not concerned with a transcendent ego that figures in the Cartesian tradition, or with the indivisibility of the soul that interested Platonists, or with the relation of the essential human form to the body that became the center of the debate among Aristotelians. He does, once in the *Pensées,* speak of the soul as something that exists in a way that takes the body beyond the material order. He tells us that there are philosophers who have "subdued their passions" and claims that no material things could do that.[61] But this is a not very characteristic piece of causal analysis that suggests a Platonic view of a soul so arranged that what controls the passions must be some different kind of thing. I think a more serious consideration is that our existence in the three orders means that while in one sense our prospects for immortality are enhanced, in another our condition is rendered more precarious. Since we do have a place in the intellectual order, there is an idea of each of us that is part of that order and is so eternally. More importantly, we have a place in the moral order. This means that if God exists, is moral, and is the omnipotent master of all the orders, then, as beings in the moral order, our existence has a permanent moral significance. Yet, to be human, we must also function in a physical order— our own or some other.[62] And in our immediate physical order, we are certainly mortal. This might give us a further reason to bet on Pascal's God since, in any case, our long-range future would seem to depend on the existence and good will of powers that are not clearly evident in our world.

The difficulty with the argument thus presented is that there might be other things one should be doing, and they might not to be consistent with believing in Pascal's God. This difficulty is heightened by the oddity of Pascal's God. Indeed, Pascal's God may be so difficult to understand that we cannot clearly identify those propositions that conflict with belief in him. Pascal does not hide the difficulties, nor does he inflate them. He is, surely, only facing the facts as Christianity presents them. God appeared fully human as Jesus only once and in one place. Why did he choose that place and time? Why did he, in the first place, choose the Jews? Why did he later decide to address the Gentiles?[63]

There are no answers. Furthermore, although Pascal is not always perfectly clear, no one reading all the passages in which Pascal discusses the human peril of damnation would conclude that Pascal thinks that God, even though he created the world and has the power to create the conditions under which virtually everyone might be saved, will probably save virtually everyone.[64]

Thus a wager on Pascal's God seems not very rational except in one circumstance. The *possibilities* for the human *"infini rien"* do include some relation to an infinite being who is capable of appearing in all three orders. If one accepts this claim of Pascal's *and* one has, anyhow, a kind of inner compulsion—one might think of it as a powerful religious urge—to believe that a certain kind of Christian God exists, then it might be reasonable to assuage one's religious feelings by betting on this God. This may have been Pascal's position.

But we do not know whether Pascal was reasonable or not unless we examine the alternatives that were open to him and ask ourselves how they would have seemed to him. Within the Judeo-Christian tradition there are two choices that fall within the ambit of many of Pascal's beliefs. One is acceptance of neo-Platonism. Forms of it have animated major strands of the tradition from the time of the Church fathers and even as far back as Philo and some of the sources of the New Testament. Some form of it was never far out of sight at Port-Royal. Martin de Barcos,[65] a major figure at Port-Royal, held an interesting version of it. The second alternative is to believe in the rather generous (if, in a sense, rule-loving) deity favored by Pascal's Jesuit opponents. That tradition, too, has roots in Judaism as well as in Christianity.

Barcos thinks it reasonable to suppose that God's mercy is as great as his justice and that, given what we believe (on evidence of Scripture) about what sorts of people are saved, it is very likely that serious believers will be saved. Barcos writes:

> As to those who say: "If I am one of the Reprobate, why should I act virtuously?" I would reply . . . : "Are you not cruel towards yourself if you destine yourself to the greatest of all evils without knowing whether God has destined you to it? He has not revealed to you His secret counsel as to your salvation or damnation. Why do you expect punishment from His justice rather than forgiveness from His Mercy? Perhaps He will accord you His grace and perhaps He will not. Why therefore do you not have as much hope as fear, instead of falling into despair about a gift which He grants to others who are just as unworthy as you? By your despair you infallibly lose what you will probably gain if you hope. And, in your doubt as to whether you are one of the Reprobate, you conclude that you should act as if you are damned already, instead of doing what might perhaps save you from damnation. Surely this is as much against the reason which you possess as a wise man as against the faith which you hold as a Christian?"[66]

This passage does have a certain odd ring to it. One might take it to suggest that bad actions will certainly land you in hell, whereas good actions will not save you. Like other Jansenists and, for that matter, virtually all seventeenth-century believers who thought of themselves as orthodox Christians, Barcos supposed that only God can save any of us. We cannot save ourselves.

Orthodoxy has it, however, that the saved will behave well, even though it is not because of their good behavior that they are saved. Hence, those who behave badly are presumably not saved. Barcos' letter suggests that some who might have been saved miss salvation by choosing to behave badly. This would suggest that we can cause God to change his mind. What this illustrates is that, short of the solution that insists that God means to save us by our free will and so has chosen from all eternity to choose what we choose, it is very difficult to get any statement that does not end in a welter of contradictions. The Jansenists and their opponents argued constantly over such questions as whether God's grace can be resisted or rejected.

Pascal had his own solution, perhaps provoked by the unclarity of people like Barcos, and I return to this later. Here, it is important to realize that it is not always clear just how one might best render Barcos' theology consistent. But despite his distrust of *human* reason, it would be wrong to follow those commentators who suppose Barcos to have been an antirationalist. A careful reading of his letter of 5 December 1652 to Mère Angélique, Antoine Arnauld's sister and the Abbess of Port-Royal, undermines the antirationalist interpretation. He does, indeed, tell Mère Angélique that "[as] there is a wisdom which is folly in the eye of God so also is there an order which is disorder; so that there is a folly which is wisdom and a disorder that shows true order." And he praises her "for the ease with which you allow your mind to wander from the laws of human reason, placing no other limits upon it but those of charity, which has no limits when it is perfect and yet too many when it is weak."[67]

Lucien Goldmann sees these words as embodying Barcos' distrust of reason, although Barcos distrusts only "human reason."[68] Human reason tends to be tied to human language into which error naturally falls. But the human mind is not wholly unreceptive to divine reason, for, fallen or not, we are created in the image of God and share in the divine reason. Human reason is, I think, for Barcos, chiefly practical reason devoted to human ends—a problem raised, after all, by Antoine Arnauld and Pierre Nicole in the "Port-Royal Logic."[69]

Naturally, as a good Augustinian Platonist, Barcos thinks that divine reason must everywhere reign supreme. But this is not to say that we have no access to it. Light is shed on this question in Barcos' *Les sentimens de M. de St. Cyran sur l'oraison mentale.*[70] Although Jean Orcibal thinks that it was written as a critique of a kind of intellectualism Barcos found at Port-Royal in the thought of Mère Angélique herself,[71] Barcos' anti-intellectualism is surely not obvious— and the rather deftly intellectualized neo-Platonism *is* quite clear.

The bulk of Barcos' book is a dialogue between a lady in a religious order— called simply *"La Religieuse"* in the Anvers (Antwerp) edition but *"Philogie"* in the Cologne edition—and Barcos himself, who uses the name St. Cyran in the Anvers edition and *"Philérème"* in the Cologne edition.[72] Certainly *"La Religieuse"* (Mère Angélique?) is being corrected about various matters. Barcos begins by saying that prayer is not a kind of sermon in which one argues with God.[73] And he says later that we do not confront God "face to face." But this is because his divinity is to be found within us ("Sa divinité . . . étant toute dans nous").[74] In short, we seek a kind of mystical union, not an argument.

But if one thinks that this kind of mysticism is anti-intellectual, one should notice that in laying down the foundation of his position, he says, "God is nothing other than truth and justice." ("Dieu n'est autre chose que verité et justice."[75]) And he adds, "Toute autre présence de Dieu peut tromper." Every other claim about the "God within" can fool us. The mystical union is, after all, with truth and justice.

Based on Barcos' view, in short, one can bet on the existence of God with a good deal of assurance. One is betting on truth and justice, and once again, the general pattern of the arguments is that even if we do not know fully what truth and justice are, our very dissatisfaction is evidence that truth and justice really exist. Furthermore, if God exists, the odds on one's being saved are probably fairly good—perhaps very good if God's mercy is really as infinite as his justice. Here it is not just (as in Pascal's argument) the magnitude of the possible good result but the probability of attaining it that helps make the bet a good one.

But it would seem that Barcos' "truth and justice" and his "God within" are not exactly the unpredictable being who is wholly other than us, in whom Pascal seems to suppose that Christians do or ought to believe. Notice that the elements of the developing kinds of neo-Platonism are here, too. It is through *us* that God expresses himself, and God is manifest as a principle—in truth and justice. It would seem that we are necessary to God's appearance in this world, and it would seem also that truth and justice are principles that precede things. Truth, therefore, is not the scientific truth extracted from a nature empty of God—a nature Pascal thought he had turned up in the vacuum experiments. Barcos offers a way of improving the odds, but because it goes, I suspect, in Pascal's view, against both science and revealed religion, he would not have found it acceptable.

There is, in addition, an important distinction between Barcos and Pascal over humanity's relation to the world. The more marked neo-Platonist position of Barcos led him to urge at least a partial withdrawal from the world. This was a position that he held in common with the *"solitaires"* of Port-Royal, whose very name, Louis Cognet says, indicates their insistence on existence both austere and "absolutely separated from the world." Pascal never became a *solitaire* and, as Cognet notes, never gave up the notion that one should work in and on the world.[76] His will reminds us of his concern for the Paris bus system and for the charities that he expects its proceeds to support.

Barcos and the *solitaires* took a different view partly, at least in the case of Barcos of himself, because of the implications of the kind of neo-Platonism to which he subscribed. The doctrine of emanation implies that the world gets further and further from God. If science finds no sign of the "return to the One," then one might suppose that the world is to be abandoned. This view is underlined if one sees the "Fall of man" as implying the corruption of the natural world.

The abandonment of the world, however, is an ambiguous doctrine. Partly it means personal withdrawal from it in the hope of making better contact with God, and partly it means leaving the world to its own doom. Lucien Goldmann speaks of Barcos' "straightforward refusal of the world" while also noticing that Barcos accepts almsgiving and helping people in danger of death as acts good in themselves.[77] In fact, Barcos accepts personal withdrawal, but he recognizes limits to the doctrine that one should leave the world entirely to its doom. Pascal also certainly thinks the blandishments of worldly pleasures should be resisted but does not advocate withdrawal in either sense.

Even with respect to personal withdrawal, there is a problem for Pascal. For Pascal's account of believing in God is tied to moral action, and he insists that the human being must be expressed in the ordinary physical world, and so involvement with its mundane details is inevitable.

To understand just why Pascal disagrees with Barcos, one must consider his rather special view about the relation of God to human beings. His *Écrits sur la grace* have a single continuing theme: Neither the Calvinists who think everything predestined nor the Molinists (and Pelagians) who believe that all the grace necessary for salvation is given to everyone are right. He says, "[Let us] defend . . . the power of grace against the Lutherans and the necessity of grace against the Pelagians without destroying free will with grace like the Lutherans or grace with free will like the Pelagians."[78]

The true doctrine is the one Pascal believes to have been enunciated by St. Augustine: Adam and Eve had original natures that guaranteed their salvation, but the Fall changed that. After the Fall, human beings were not necessarily damned, but their condition was perilous. So God sent Jesus to save them. In this process God made some choices. Some people remained damned because they could not, by their natures, respond to the new grace. Some still cannot respond. Why this should be so is a mystery not known to us. Others could respond and "were called," but among these, some persevered and some did not. It is still the case that many are called, but not all persevere.

In its turn, this doctrine to be orthodox has to be understood in some way so that God is not to blame for anyone's damnation. He is responsible for the salvation of those who are saved. For if he is omnipotent and he intends to save anyone, he must, surely, succeed. Pascal gives the answer in the first few pages of the manuscript. His solution is based on some quotations from St. Paul's letters to the Galatians, the Ephesians, and the Romans. When we are saved, God "lives in us"; our will and God's become in some way fused. Thus, what we will, God wills. When we are damned there is a distinction between the two wills. The distinction is a negation, a lack. God, who is wholly positive, is not responsible for this.[79]

But if God acts in and through me and I am in the world, then God acts in the world. It is not, therefore, through withdrawing from the world that God is to be encountered, but by acting in it. Emanationist neo-Platonism of the sort espoused by Barcos carries with it the implicit notion that in withdrawing from the world I can move to the level of prior emanations, which are nearer to God than the world. But, evidently, that is not how Pascal's God works.

If we follow Pascal and reject Barcos' God, what then of the deity envisaged by the Jesuits? Might it not be better to bet on *him?* The Jesuit whose thought most interestingly connects and contrasts with Pascal's, perhaps, is René Rapin. Just two years older than Pascal (Rapin was born at Tours in 1621, joined the Jesuit order in 1639, and died in Paris in 1687), he was a young man about town, well known in literary circles, when Pascal was writing. More importantly, he compiled an account, filling eighteen folio-sized notebooks, on the Jansenist controversy.[80] Pascal and Barcos did battle openly with the Jesuits François Annat and Antoine Sirmond, but these two, I think, were a little more cautious than Rapin.

Rapin wrote a great many books on literature and on religion, often one on each every year. (A popular quip had it that he "served God and man by semester.") Pascal did not change Rapin's mind. In his *L'Importance du salut,* he has a chapter entitled "Qu'il n'est pas difficile de se sauver."[81] Despite that, Rapin found much to admire in Pascal. He called him "an extraordinary man, a man of vast spirit and profound penetration" and "the man with the most admirable genius for mathematics in the century."[82] Pascal, however, showed no signs of understanding scholastic theology and therefore, Rapin thought, should not have disputed fine points with the doctors of theology. Rapin faults Pascal for his lack of understanding of moral theory and its problems, and he claims that by the end of the *Provincial Letters* Pascal has descended into *"bouffonneries."*[83] In the nature of things, the passages in Rapin's *Mémoires* devoted to Pascal are concerned with replying to the *Provincial Letters* and with showing the reasonableness of much Jesuit thought and the need to make fine distinctions in moral theory, but Rapin refers to the *Pensées* as *"ce bel ouvrage."*

In his own work, however, Rapin argues that God did not create us in order to have something to vent his anger upon (Rapin adopts in essence the very doctrine of which Pascal makes fun[84]), but in order to save us. Naturally, God will provide ways within our means for our salvation and will take account of our circumstances and our frailties.

The God of Rapin has clear aims, intends to succeed in them, and has granted himself every power needed to do so. The claim that it is difficult or impossible for us to ensure our own salvation is well founded, for human beings have many weaknesses. Yet the title of one of his chapters still says it is not difficult to save oneself *("de se sauver")*. God does the work if we will let him *and* if we follow the most basic rules, the most important of which is that we must always work for the salvation of others. For it is by showing the concern for others that God shows for us that we best and most easily come to express the divine spirit. To be saved, we need to let the divine spirit express itself through us. This is also the central message of his *L'Esprit du Christianisme*.[85] There he says that the essence of the true spirit of Christianity is charity.

One does have to follow the rules, though Rapin sees the rules in a large and latitudinarian way and paints God as well aware of human weakness. And, in the face of God's determination, one would have to be very determined (like Satan perhaps) or very careless not to be saved. Such a God seems to be a still better bet, for one must remember that Pascal is asking us to invest in a whole life of directed activity, and yet he admits that his God may well reject it all because it is difficult to say just what he expects or even how he would react if he received what he expected. From what Rapin tells us about his God, one might conclude that there is very little chance that one's efforts as a believer will fail if Rapin's God exists, certainly if one is sincere.

Since both Rapin and Pascal urge active commitment to human charity, one might think the investment in either bet would be the same, indeed, that it would be difficult to know whether one was betting on one God or on the other. But this is not quite so. If we take Pascal seriously when he tells us to treat all human beings as saved, we presumably run into the problem of human authority and the question of what to do with human wrongdoers who imperil society. Rapin's instruction is to treat them charitably, but Pascal, if he is to be taken literally, would demand something stronger than this. Working out a theory of social order to Pascal's specifications might be no small matter.

More obviously, there is clearly a difference in anxiety levels. Pascal wants us to worry constantly about the dark God who urged Abraham to sacrifice his son Isaac and whose behavior in picking a "chosen people" (whether only once or from time to time) to receive revelations seems to defy explanation. Pascal tells us often enough not to expect God to explain all his doings to us and not to expect to know who is saved. Rapin's God has a nature that makes it likely that he will do so much to save us that we will have to be quite determined to avoid him. Bluntly, Pascal asks more of us and expects less of God.

Thus, the investment needed for Rapin's bet seems likely to be smaller. Pascal is one of those, never rare in religious life, whose conscience rebels against the notion of easy salvation. But any modern utilitarian would surely perceive the merits of Rapin's position.

Is Rapin's *really* the better bet? It would be if the initial evidence for the existence of Rapin's God were better than the evidence for Pascal's God. But in

Pascal's terms, the evidence for the existence of Rapin's God is very shaky. Indeed it is, he would say, shakier than the evidence for the neo-Platonist God's existence, which can be deduced, if one accepts the emanationist reading, from the existence of the infinite, per se, something Pascal accepts. Pascal's complaint about such a God is chiefly empirical. Nature, physical nature at any rate, does not clearly testify to the existence of this God. But Pascal would be willing, I think, to argue the point.

The grounds for taking Rapin's God seriously, however, are essentially deductions from the Jesuitical interpretation of Scripture, the testimony of the saints, and at least a tincture of the medieval (generally Aristotelian) philosophers, whose God, being Aristotelian, was logical in a clearly understood sense.[86] Pascal has no use for the philosophy of the "schools" and less for the Jesuitical readings of Scripture.

Obviously, however, what is and is not a good bet among these options depends on one's choices. If one accepts more of the neo-Platonist argument, the God of Barcos is a good bet. Also, if one reads Scripture and accepts an optimistic account of the capabilities of man and a view according to which God is intelligible, rational, powerful, and very much determined to save all those who really want to be saved, then Rapin's God is a better bet. Perhaps most of all, Rapin's God is to be argued for in historical terms.

In determining what Christianity is, Rapin relies on the continuity of a tradition embodied in the Church as an institution. If one were to take even the critical (but not completely skeptical) position of La Mothe le Vayer about history, one might incline to Rapin's God. And we should notice that Rapin's outlook, like La Mothe le Vayer's, is fundamentally shaped by a literary tradition derived from writings of classical antiquity.[87]

Outside the rather cosy confines of this literary tradition—a tradition that had humanized Christianity and rendered it both more comfortable to authority and more certain to the believer—Christianity takes on a more puzzling air. For Pascal, whose certainties, such as they were, were scientific and mathematical, Christianity appeared more startlingly paradoxical, and seen from the Jansenist perspective of men and women who were suspicious of a comfortable Christianity, it was bound to seem more demanding. Thus Pascal takes the position he does largely because, for him, scientific knowledge and the claims of morality are the conjoint bases of the decisions of serious men and women.

These, then, are options within what one might think of as the Christian tradition of the time. But we can see the most basic issues only if we pose the question more generally. What, then, are the other options?

The most obvious, of course, is that nothing like any of the Gods we have talked about exists, and there is not, either, anything that we might think of as an objective "validating principle" for the claim to be *"infini"* as well as *"rien."*

But in Pascal's view, the very existence of the concept of the infinite tells against this option. We ought to encourage the skeptic to press the case as forcefully as possible, for this is the condition of intellectual honesty that makes the enquiry worthwhile in any case. Yet the skeptic who insists that every proposition can be rejected is insisting precisely that the human being is not a "thinking machine," for the thinking machine can never reject all of its programs and still be a thinking machine.

This tells heavily against the claim that there is no reality beyond the simple physical reality, and yet it creates the situation that makes it clear that we must bet. Yet, if we think of a God who has no personal characteristics at all and stick as close as we can to the claims of a scientific world outlook—an outlook that Pascal also takes to be sound—we can still accommodate the infinite. In purely intellectual terms, at any rate, this might well seem more plausible than a system that includes the "God of Abraham and Isaac." It is the idea of the infinite itself that gives such scope and power to mathematics (allowing it to transcend in various ways many postulated limitations). Theories that proceed in this direction include, of course, various Hindu conceptions of Brahman and pagan Neoplatonist concepts of the One. They include notions such as the neo-Confucian idea of T'ien which is simply "the heavenly principle" separated as much as possible from every attempt to give it the shape of a person. Malebranche worried extensively about the possibility that this principle is a serious competitor to his own ideas of God.[88] The simplest account of Malebranche's answer is that a perfect principle that represents the infinite capacities of every possible world would, if it were perfectly instantiated, result in the existence of the most perfect being imaginable—that is, the God Malebranche (but not Pascal) takes to be the Christian God. Malebranche is quite willing to suppose that his God is subordinated always to principle.

Such a being would need our cooperation to exist in our world, and I think this is in any case implied in Malebranche's philosophy. It was altogether acceptable to his disciple Yves-Marie André. All such schemes have much in common with the notions of Barcos and are really encompassed in the notion that what really does exist is something objectively called the infinite that interacts with our finite world in a very complex way. In fact, if it is true that one must bet, this theory would seem to be the best bet. One who bets on it, certainly, should always have in mind that this is, indeed, no more than a bet. Reason suggests that something instantiates the infinite. Our natures as knowing—and doubting—beings do seem to involve us with the concept of infinity. Perhaps nothing counts as a proof, but nothing seems likely to rescue us from our association with infinity either.

A philosophy like that of André (or perhaps of Crousaz) would make most sense of such a notion. But many modern men and women, like Pascal, find such an idea very difficult to accept, for it seems difficult to reconcile with the claims of traditional religions such as Christianity, Judaism, and Islam and equally difficult to square with the claims of science. Postmodern thought promises to free us from science, bourgeois rationality, and traditional religion alike, but it does not seem to give us a way of facing up to the infinite and seems unlikely to cater to neo-Platonist tastes.

But anyone who thinks that we are not simply mechanisms in a complex physical and economic system still has to bet. For if we are not fully programmed, we have to choose, and no final certainties seem to be forthcoming.

NOTES
WORKS CITED
INDEX

NOTES

Introduction

1. Henri Gouhier, *Blaise Pascal, conversion et apologétique* (Paris: J. Vrin, 1986), 149.

2. Throughout this monograph, I use *neo-Platonism* to identify all the strands of thought, which though they have a marked Platonic coloring, nevertheless show the signs of later developments. I use *Neoplatonism* in its conventional sense to denote philosophy fairly closely associated with Plotinus and subsequent developments of *his* philosophy and of the philosophers who had much in common with him.

3. Port-Royal is certainly associated with Jansenism, but one must remember that Jansen's *Augustinus* did not appear until 1640 in Louvain and 1641 in Paris. Activity at Port-Royal goes back to 1608. The impact of Bérulle was very extensive, as Jean Orcibal has shown. See his *Duvergier de Hauranne, abbé de Saint-Cyran et son temps*, 2 vols. (Paris: J. Vrin, 1947).

4. LD 174, B 79, LL 84; LD 297, B 78, LL 887. Descartes is called "uncertain" as well as "troublesome."

1. Pascal, the Wager, and the Background

1. LD 343, B 233, LL 418.

2. LD 435, B 751, LL 228.

3. What I mean by "best understood" will become clearer as the argument goes on. But I cheerfully concede that many of Pascal's fragments lack a demonstrably unique meaning. I argue that the historical context, the conditions that any possible "Christian apologetic" would have been expected to meet, and what we know of Pascal's character and of the workings of his mind in other matters make some readings much more likely than others. Where all else fails, one should, of course, try to read any philosopher in a way that proves philosophically interesting, although this does not always lead to a historically accurate reading.

4. LD 435, B 751, LL 228. Pierre de Bérulle had said that God was "hidden as a man," but Pascal does not say this is the *only* guise of God. The idea is a very old one in Christian theology.

5. LD 246, B 434, LL 131.

6. This is the burden of the part of LD 246, B 434, and LL 131 that reads, "If man had never been corrupted he would enjoy . . . truth and happiness" and that "We have an idea of happiness . . . and perceive an image of truth," even though they seem to be beyond our grasp.

7. LD 11, B 194, LL 427.

8. Pascal calls them the intellect, the body, and charity (LD 585, B 793, LL 308).

9. LD 309, B 430, LL 149.

10. Pascal insists in LD 4, B 22, LL 523 that what is original in the *Pensées* is to be found in the order.

11. Ian Hacking, "The Logic of Pascal's Wager," *American Philosophical Quarterly* 9 (1972): 186–92.

12. Peter C. Dalton, "Pascal's Wager, the First Argument," *International Journal for the Philosophy of Religion* 7 (1976): 346–68, and "Pascal's Wager, the Second Argument," *Southern Journal of Philosophy* 13 (1975): 31–46.

13. P. T. Landsberg, "Gambling on God," *Mind*, n.s. 80 (1971): 100–104.

14. Terence Penelhum, "Pascal's Wager," *Journal of Religion* 44 (1964): 201–9.

15. Nicholas Rescher, *Pascal's Wager* (Notre Dame: Notre Dame University Press, 1985), 89.

16. Rescher, 74–78 and 108–13. I argue that Rescher is wrong about Pascal, but a good case can

be made for the proposition that John Tillotson (1630–94) proposed a wager in terms that make Rescher's analysis quite appropriate. Tillotson's sermon, *The Wisdom of Being Religious,* was originally published as a pamphlet at the request of the aldermen of the City of London (London: S. Gellibrand, 1664). The wager discussion appears on 30–37. It was preached at St. Paul's during or just before March 1663 so that Tillotson would not have known about Pascal's wager. Tillotson specifically addresses his readers' interests. He insists, like Rescher, however, that it is not "worldly interests" that are "at issue."

17. See Immanuel Kant, *Critique of Practical Reason* (1788), trans. Lewis White Beck (New York: Liberal Arts Press, 1956), 114.

18. Rescher, 120.

19. Rescher, 99.

20. Rescher, 97.

21. Rescher, ix.

22. Rescher, 117–19.

23. For the details of Lachelier's argument, see Jules Lachelier in "Notes on the *Pari* de Pascal," trans. and included in Edward G. Ballard, ed., *The Philosophy of Jules Lachelier* (The Hague: Martinus Nijhoff, 1960), 97–111. Lachelier thought that the bet was intended to be attractive to all human beings and to lead away from their present states. It would thus, of course, transcend their apparent self-interest but make them recognize a new interest in transcendent goods.

24. LD 313, B 477/606, LL 617; LD 418, B 492, LL 617. *Self-love (amour-propre)* occurs twelve times in the *Pensées* and is always condemned. *Concupiscence* occurs forty-six times and is used in a very general sense, with exceptions such as the reference to *"concupiscence de la chair"* (LD 721, B 460, LL 933). *Self-love* and *concupiscence* are linked in LD 302, B 544, LL 460. (The figures for frequencies are taken from Hugh M. Davidson and Pierre H. Dubé, *Concordance to Pascal's Pensées* [Ithaca: Cornell University Press, 1975].)

25. See, for instance, LD 391, B 347, LL 200.

26. LD 585, B 793, LL 308.

27. LD 224, B 277, LL 423.

28. See the discussion of this kind of insight in Keith Arnold's essay, "Pascal's Great Experiment," *Dialogue* 28 (1989): 401–15.

29. Matthew Arnold, *St. Paul and Protestantism* (London: Smith, Elder, 1870), included in volume 6 of R. H. Super's *Prose Works of Matthew Arnold* (Ann Arbor: University of Michigan Press, 1968). The Resurrection is discussed at some length in volume 6, *Dissent and Dogma,* 47–55.

30. LD 2, B 274, LL 530.

31. Pascal's *Lettres Provinciales* were first published in Paris in 1656. They are now easily available in many editions, especially Jean Steinmann's (Paris: Armand Colin, 1962), which has the response of the Jesuit Gabriel Daniel bound with it.

32. See Léon Brunschvicg, *Blaise Pascal* (Paris: Rieder, 1932), 49–52; and Jacques Chevalier, *Pascal* (Paris: Plon, 1923), 249–61.

33. See chapter 5.

34. Skeptics, referred to almost always as *"pyrrhoniens,"* are mentioned in twenty-three *pensées.* I analyze these texts in chapter 5. The word *libertin* does not occur in the *Pensées. Libertinage* occurs twice (LD 364, B 256, LL 179; LD 779, B 956, LL 952). In the first passage, Pascal says that there are not many "true" Christians. Many believe through superstition, and others do not believe because they are influenced by *libertinage.* Real Christians belong to neither group. The second mention is in a note about the Jesuits and is connected with the *Provincial Letters.* It simply suggests that the search for an "accommodating religion" is "une cherche par libertinage"; that is, it involves freethinking of an undesirable kind.

35. LD 295, B 432, LL 691.

36. Terence Penelhum, *God and Skepticism* (Dordrecht: D. Reidel, 1983).

37. LD 246, B 434, LL 131.

38. Per Lønning, *Cet effrayant pari,* literally, *This Terrifying Bet* (Paris: J. Vrin, 1980), 152–153. Lønning's title is adapted from a remark by François René de Chateaubriand, who spoke not of *"le*

pari" but of Pascal himself—*"cet effrayant genie"* ("Genie du christianisme," chap. 6 in *Oeuvres,* vol. 2 [Paris: Garnier, 1859], 13).

39. Henri Gouhier, *Blaise Pascal, Commentaire* (Paris: J. Vrin, 1966, 1984), 287–306.

40. LD 218, B 397, LL 114.

41. LD 174, B 79, LL 84; LD 297, B 78, LL 887.

2. The Platonic Elements in the Historical Context

1. LD 343, B 233, LL 418.

2. In LD 246, B 434, LL 131, Pascal states the opposition; in LD 213, B 392, LL 109, he insists again that the natural light of reason is opposed to skepticism. In LD 98, B 390, LL 896, he assures us that skepticism is sound when we consider our knowledge of *this* (our) world (especially in the light of the possibilities for salvation or damnation).

3. LD 47, B 61, LL 694.

4. LD 47, B 61, LL 694. The order seems to be the natural order, but the complaint is that mathematics is, in a sense, too profound for us.

5. In LD 922, B 91, LL 660, Pascal says that nature can deceive us, but in the same fragment, he insists that nature does not always follow her own rules.

6. François de la Mothe le Vayer was (almost certainly) born in Paris in 1588 and died in 1672. Chapter 5 contains a more detailed account of his work. Some of his best-known views are laid out in his *Dialogues faits à l'imitation des anciens,* probably first published in Frankfurt by J. Sarius in the 1630s, although the exact date is uncertain.

7. LD 70, B 374, LL 33.

8. This admission is surely a central pillar of the wager fragment (LD 343, B 233, LL 418).

9. For Pascal's views on the infinite in various contexts, see LD 260, B 532, LL 500; LD 268, B 469, LL 135; LD 344, B 231, LL 420; LD 348, B 232, LL 682; and LD 390, B 72, LL 199.

10. LD 343, B 233, LL 418.

11. Both *infini* and *infinité* exist as nouns in French now and did so in Pascal's time. *Infini,* of course, can also function as an adjective, but the juxtaposition with *rien* (which is always a noun) suggests that it is a noun in this case, although the words stand alone. Of the forty-four instances of *infini* in the *Pensées,* nineteen are nouns preceded by an article. There are also twenty-two instances of the feminine *infinie,* all of which, of course, are adjectives. Pascal uses *infinité* some twenty-three times. The Larousse *Lexis,* the most commonly used French etymological dictionary (Paris: Librairie Larousse, 1975), suggests that *infini* is normally used in mathematics, philosophy, and religion to indicate whatever is without limits. *Infinité* can have the same sense, but it was often used (at least classically) to designate the characteristic of being infinite rather than for infinity itself and, at other times, suggests only a very large quantity *(quantité extrème).* If *extrème* means something like "largest imaginable," we might think it and the unlimited were the same, but the editors offer as an example *"l'infinité d'argent qui se donne à tous les états"*—which surely cannot be a mathematical infinite. Pascal's uses of *infinité* often suggest only a "large quantity" of things, propositions, and so forth. (Frequencies of occurrence are taken from Davidson and Dubé's *Concordance.*)

12. Matthew 27.46; Mark 15.34.

13. Blaise Pascal, *Oeuvres complètes,* ed. Jacques Chevalier (Paris: Gallimard, Pléiade, 1954), 483–86. This letter is important, and more of its details are considered in chapter 3.

14. LD 344, B 231, LL 420.

15. LD 344, B 231, LL 420.

16. Because approval of St. Philip Neri's original Italian order was delayed by the Pope, Bérulle was the founder of the first official Oratorian order. His complex web of human relationships tied him to Descartes himself, among many others.

17. Bérulle's most important philosophical thoughts are in *Discours de l'éstat et des grandeurs de Jésus* (Paris: A. Estiene, 1623). There are several editions of his complete works.

18. Bérulle, *Discours,* 115. Copernicus is praised for having the courage to insist that the earth

is not the center of the universe. Similarly, in theology, the human individual is not the center of the universe, God is.

19. Pascal spells it *"Infiny rien"* with a capital *I* and no punctuation on the manuscript line in which these are the only words. See the "palaeographic edition" of the *Pensées* edited by Zacharie Tourneur (Paris: J. Vrin, 1942), 307. This is based on Bibliothèque Nationale MS. 9202, known as *"le recueil original."* Louis Lafuma and others believe that MS. 9203, known as *"la copie,"* more likely keeps Pascal's original order, but 9202, whatever is to be said about its order, contains what we have in Pascal's own hand (see the Note on Texts). There is a photographic reprint (not very clear) of the wager fragment in Lønning, *Cet effrayant pari.*

20. See Pierre de Bérulle, *Oeuvres de Cardinal Bérulle,* ed. François Bourgoing (Paris: Antoine Estiene and Sebastien Huré, 1644).

21. Bérulle, *Opuscules de pieté,* CX, and *De la présence réelle du corps de Jésus en la saincte Eucharistie,* in *Oeuvres,* 104–6.

22. Bérulle, *Discours,* 138; *Oeuvres,* 192–93.

23. LD 737, LL 913 (not numbered in B): Pascal's account of his own experience. Here Pascal feels himself consumed by fire and separated from God, and it is revealed to him, apparently, that truth comes only through Scripture.

24. Yves de Paris' works include: *La Théologie naturelle ou les premières véritez de foy eclaircies par raisons sensibles et moralles,* 4 vols. (Paris: Nicolas Buon, 1633, 1640); *De l'indifférence* (Paris: Thierry, 1638; reprint, Paris: Belles-Lettres, 1966); *Très-humbles remonstrances presentées à la reine contre les nouvelles doctrines de ce temps* (Paris, 1644); *Digestum Sapientiae,* vol. 1 (Paris: Thierry, 1648), and vol. 2 (1654); and *L'Agent de Dieu dans le monde* (Paris: Thierry, 1656). *(Yves is Ives in the 1633 edition of Théologie naturelle, but Yves afterwards. The British Library and institutions that follow it retain Ives for his entries.)*

25. Yves de Paris, *Très-humbles remonstrances.*

26. Charles Chesneau [also known as Julien-Eymard d'Angers] in his *Le Père Yves de Paris et son temps,* 2 vols. (Paris: Societé de l'Histoire Ecclésiastique de la France, 1946) devotes a good deal of space to Pascal's likely objections to Yves, although in fact, despite Yves' prominence and his specific involvement in polemics against Port-Royal, there is no evidence that Pascal actually read him.

27. Frank E. Manuel remarks that Newton's "world system has a cast that is Platonic . . . Newton conceived of the ontological problem of causation within a traditional neo-Platonic framework" (*A Portrait of Isaac Newton* [London: Frederick Muller, 1980]). But this does not mean that Newton's philosophy and that of Yves de Paris are identical, and one should notice that, although Newtonian science can be accommodated to Yves' scheme, some of Newton's personal religious views cannot. In his chapter entitled "Newton's Scientific Theism," in *Hume, Newton, and the Design Argument* (Lincoln: University of Nebraska Press, 1965), Robert H. Hurlbutt III gives a good account of the neo-Platonist ideas in what one should call Newton's philosophical theology. But Manuel, after patient sifting through much of the manuscript material that Newton left behind, leaves no doubt that Newton dislikes some central theological implications of emanationism and very frequently insists on regarding God not as the principle of goodness in things but as the ruler of the world. Thus the relation of Newton's theological views to his scientific theories remains clouded. (See Frank E. Manuel, *The Religion of Isaac Newton* [Oxford: The Clarendon Press, 1974].)

28. *Moralles* here is used in sense II, i, "having to do with the intellect," *Grande Larousse,* vol. 4 (Paris: Librairie Larousse, 1977).

29. See, e.g., 1: 124–25, of the 1640 edition of Yves' *Théologie naturelle.*

30. Chesneau, *Le Père Yves.* The notion that "nature abhors a vacuum" suggests that being permeates everything. If God made the world, he presumably included no unnecessary evils. If evil is always a lack of something, an empty space that could be filled would tell against God's existence, while a world with no emptiness would provide some evidence that God exists. Based on Pascal's view though, it is simply air that fills space and creates the illusion that vacuums do not exist. See *Le Vide, l'équilibre des liqueurs et la pesanteur de l'air,* in *Oeuvres,* ed. Chevalier, 412–57. Pascal says, "la masse de l'air . . . est la véritable et unique cause" (457).

31. Yves discusses these matters in a number of places, especially *Théologie naturelle,* vols. 1 and 3.

32. Yves, *Théologie naturelle*, 1640 edition, 1:521–22.

33. Yves puts this thesis forward in his *L'Agent de Dieu dans le monde*.

34. Descartes' letter to Marin Mersenne, 11 November 1640 *(Oeuvres,* AT, III:231–32; Alquié, II:273–77). (AT refers to the edition of Charles Adam and Paul Tannery, revised under the direction of the Centre Nationale de la Recherche Scientifique [Paris: J. Vrin, 1971]. Alquié refers to the edition of Ferdinand Alquié [Paris: Garnier, 1973].)

35. Eustachius' works include: *Summa Philosophiae Quadrapartita* (Paris: C. Chastellain, 1609 [*Chastellain* is spelled *Chastelain* in the 1613 edition]; Cambridge: Roger Daniels, 1640); *Summa Theologiae Tripartita* (Paris: Carolus Chastelain [with *one l*], 1613–16); and *Exercices spirituels contenant plusieurs méditations* (Paris: M. du Puis, 1630; and various other editions to 1640).

36. Eustachius, *Physica*, in *Summa Philosophiae,* Cambridge edition, 154–55. (The major works within the *Summa*—*Physica, Metaphysica,* etc.—are numbered separately in nearly all editions, but the Cambridge edition has *Physica* and *Ethica* numbered consecutively.) Page numbers given in these notes are numbers within the appropriate subwork.

37. See Descartes' letters to Marin Mersenne, 11 November 1640 and 22 December 1641 (AT, III:231–32; AT, III:470; Alquié, II:273–77); letter of 22 December 1641 (summarized in Alquié, II:903); and his letter to Denis Mesland, 9 February 1645 (AT, IV:161–75; Alquié, III:544–53). These letters contain his references to Eustachius as well as to transubstantiation. The revised AT, IV, is dated 1972.

38. Eustachius, *Summa Philosophiae,* Cambridge edition. For the notion of substance, see *Metaphysica,* 61; for the notion of transcendental truth, see *Metaphysica,* 32–33; for the role of particulars and principles, see *Physica,* 331–34.

39. In LD 343, B 233, LL 418, Pascal goes so far as to say that the finite "becomes nothing" in the presence of the infinite.

40. LD 309, B 430, LL 149; LD 674, B 538, LL 358; and LD 676, B 482, LL 360 are clear examples.

3. The Doctrine of Orders

1. I say "in a sense" because Pascal uses the notion in more than one way. Pierre Chibaudel has recently argued that one can *also* think of the orders as incompatible forms of mind or even as "societies ignoring one another" ("Sur le fragment des trois ordres de Blaise Pascal," *Archives de philosophie* 53 [1990]: 631–45). But the orders are *at least* to be conceived of as distinct realms, although I argue that the distinctness is of a special kind.

2. LD 344, B 231, LL 420.

3. Pascal, *Oeuvres,* ed. Chevalier, 483–86; *Oeuvres complètes,* ed. Jean Mesnard, vol. 2 (Paris: Desclée de Brouwer, 1970), 580–83.

4. LD 391, B 347, LL 200.

5. LD 257, B 358, LL 678.

6. LD 163, B 129, LL 641.

7. LD 162, B 94, LL 630.

8. John Locke, *An Essay Concerning Human Understanding,* bk. 4, chap. 12, sec. 8. (The *Essay* was first published in London in 1690. The standard modern edition ed. Peter H. Nidditch [Oxford: The Clarendon Press, 1975] is made from the 4th ed. [London: Awnsham and John Churchil, 1700].)

9. Locke, *Essay,* bk. 4, chap. 10.

10. Sir Arthur Eddington, *The Nature of the Physical Universe* (Cambridge: The University Press, 1927, 1930).

11. LD 47, B 61, LL 694 is headed "order," and it contains the following very dark sentence: "No human science keeps it [the order]. Mathematics keeps it, but it is useless because of its depth." It is not clear what "the order" is. Pascal says he could have ordered his work by beginning with the vanity of ordinary human lives and then gone on to deal with the philosophers, both Pyrrhonists (skeptics) and Stoics, but "the order would not have been kept." It is possible that *the order* is simply the order of his own text, but there seems no reason why he should keep *that order. The* order seems

more likely to be the order of nature. The depth of mathematics is therefore the problem. Is he also saying that mathematics is not a human science?

12. LD 343, B 233, LL 418.

13. LD 344, B 231, LL 420.

14. See the discussion in chapter 5.

15. LD 174, B 79, LL 84; LD 297, B 78, LL 887.

16. Pascal insists that miracles are no longer necessary (LD 798, B 832, LL 880) and that we do not need to be shown that we ought to love God (LD 881, B 837, LL 844), yet there is no reasonable argument against miracles (LD 473, B 815, LL 568). He says that they are necessary to address man in his entirety, in his body as well as in his mind (LD 884, B 806, LL 848). I think what this means is that miracles force us to think of various alternative orders in the world.

17. Descartes, *Oeuvres,* AT, III:663–69; Alquié, III:43–48.

18. LD 761, B 75, LL 958.

19. He called it simply "La Machine arithmétique" (*Oeuvres*, ed. Chevalier, 349–58). But he says more about it in LD 231, B 240, LL 741; and LD 585, B 793, LL 308.

20. LD 231, B 340, LL 741.

21. In LD 231, B 340, LL 741, Pascal mentions the will and the machine; in LD 585, B 793, LL 308, he asserts that matter has no thought within it.

22. LD 381, B 543, LL 190.

23. LD 174, B 79, LL 84.

24. LD 381, B 543, LL 190.

25. A. W. S. Baird, *Studies in Pascal's Ethics,* chap. 2 (The Hague: Martinus Nijhoff, 1975).

26. Lucien Goldmann, *Le Dieu caché* (Paris: Gallimard, 1955), 322ff.; trans. by Philip Thody as *The Hidden God* (London: Routledge & Kegan Paul; New York: Humanities Press, 1964), 290ff. See LD 11, B 194, LL 427.

27. LD 11, B 194, LL 427.

28. As LD 676, B 482, LL 360 puts it.

29. LD 344, B 231, LL 420.

30. Chevalier, 80–81, 181–82.

31. Baird, 86.

32. Gouhier, *Blaise Pascal, conversion et apologétique;* see especially 157. Gouhier remarks that Plato is cited in the *Pensées* for his inability to convert the pagans to monotheism. Of course, Pascal did not think Plato a substitute for religion. But this is not to say that Platonism was thought by Pascal to be false, but only that Platonism was not a substitute for Christianity.

33. John Locke, *An Examination of P. Malebranche's Opinion of seeing all Things in God,* in *Posthumous Works of Mr. John Locke* (London: W. B. for A. and J. Churchill, 1706); and *Remarks upon some of Mr. Norris's Books, wherein he asserts P. Malebranche's Opinion of seeing all Things in God,* in *A Collection of several Pieces of Mr. John Locke* (London: J. Bettesworth for R. Franklin, 1720).

34. Locke, *Remarks,* sec. 16.

35. Locke, *Examination,* sec. 42.

36. Locke, *Essay,* bk. 2, chap. 28, sec. 14; Nidditch edition, 357–59.

37. Locke, *Essay,* bk. 4, chap. 10; Nidditch edition, 619–30.

38. LD 395, B 660, LL 616; LD 141, B 455, LL 597.

39. LD 257, B 358, LL 678.

40. LD 390, B 72, LL 199.

41. LD 246, B 434, LL 131.

42. Pascal, *Oeuvres*, ed. Chevalier, 52.

43. LD 246, B 434, LL 131.

44. LD 344, B 231, LL 420. The ideas are strange enough to make it necessary to look at the French text so as to be sure the translation does not change anything. The words in brackets are not included in most modern texts, but they are in the MS. BN 9202. See Tourneur's "palaeographic edition," 312.

45. LD 308, B 488, LL 988.

4. Human Dealings with God: The Development of the Neo-Platonist Responses

1. Hence, e.g., Henri Bergson's interest in Plotinus. See Rose-Marie Mossé-Bastide, *Bergson et Plotin* (Paris: Presses Universitaires de France, 1959). But Samuel Alexander, Alfred North Whitehead, John Elof Boodin, and Teilhard de Chardin exhibit, to one degree or another, facets of the old idea of the return. The issues are a little different, but one can also read Hegel this way.

2. These issues are developed further in chapter 5. Here, I want to call attention to several ways in which Pascal approaches this theme. In LD 878, B 843, LL 840, he insists that "God and man have a mutual duty." He says "these words must be forgiven," but this does not, apparently, undermine their force, for he adds that God "owes it to men not to lead them into error." Thus, if men act, God *will* respond. Pascal's examples of these responses have to do with the way in which God acts in the world so as to confirm or disconfirm religious doctrines so that "doctrine must be judged by miracles and miracles must be judged by doctrine." A much stronger response is suggested in LD 731, B 286, LL 381, in which Pascal says, "God became man in order to unite himself with us." Ultimately, he tells us in LD 676, B 482, LL 360 that we are "a body of thinking members of God," although we are not aware of it. This is also the theme of LD 687, B 473, LL 371; and LD 688, B 483, LL 372. Thus, how one acts makes a difference to the life of God in the world. For Pascal, believing in the existence of God is an act that itself makes a difference both to us and to God. Hence the advice he gives at the end of the "wager" fragment to those who have difficulty in believing: Imitate those who do believe (LD 343, B 233, LL 418). An interesting discussion of the problem of belief is in Stephen T. Davis' "Pascal on Self-Caused Belief," *Religious Studies* 27 (1991): 27–37; but Davis does not explore the many ways in which Pascal says that God is related to us, to the world, and through us to the world. Preoccupation with this issue at the time explains the success of Jean de Rotrou's play *Le Véritable Saint Genest* (Paris: Toussainct Quinet 1647; Sand, for the Comédie Française, 1988), in which the hero, an unbeliever, plays the part of a Christian only to become a Christian and to be sentenced to death for his part.

3. Arnauld and Malebranche seem not to have been able to understand one another. The debate has recently been studied in great detail in Steven M. Nadler, *Arnauld and the Cartesian Philosophy of Ideas* (Princeton: Princeton University Press, 1989).

4. Richard A. Watson has examined Foucher in depth in *The Breakdown of Cartesian Metaphysics*, which incorporates a revised version of his earlier *Downfall of Cartesianism* (New York: Humanities Press, 1987). Just where Foucher intended to go remains somewhat doubtful. Leibniz thought quite highly of him, and it is possible to think of Foucher as trying to produce a kind of idealism with affinities to Berkeley, but he was certainly skeptical about some questions, and there is no question about his opposition to Malebranche.

5. See Yves-Marie André, *La Vie du P. Malebranche, prêtre de l'oratoire, avec l'histoire de ses ouvrages* (Paris: Ingold, 1886). André's *Essai sur le beau* (Paris: H. L. et J. Guérin, 1741; J. P. du Halde, 1744) continues to be of interest to aestheticians.

6. Jean-Henri Samuel Formey, a French theologian, who was born in Berlin of a French refugee family in 1711 and who became the great expositor of Christian Wolff, published an edition of André's *Essai sur le Beau* in 1759 (Amsterdam: J. H. Schneider). In his preface, he says Cartesian aesthetics really does derive from Crousaz (xxxi) but that André makes great improvements, above all in his account of creativity, while nevertheless giving adequate attention to the fact that *"le beau"* cannot be merely an affair of fantasy (xiv). Formey contrasts Francis Hutcheson unfavorably with André.

7. Crousaz's *Traité du beau* appeared in 1715 (Amsterdam: F. L. Honoré). After generations of neglect, it has been republished (Paris: Fayard, 1985). The three-volume edition of his *La Logique ou système de réflexions* (Amsterdam: Honoré et Châtelain, 1720) contains a clear account of his thesis about free will. The most expanded version, a six-volume edition, was published in 1741 (Lausanne and Geneva: Bousquet). Very important for our purposes is his *Examen du pyrrhonisme ancien et moderne* (The Hague: Pierre de Hondt, 1733).

8. Crousaz, *Examen*, 148.

9. Crousaz, *Examen*, 452.

10. Crousaz, *Examen*, 400.

11. Crousaz, *Traité du beau*, Fayard, 259–87.

12. Jean-Pierre de Crousaz, *Logique, abrégé* (Amsterdam: Z. Châtelain, 1737), 95–96.

13. Crousaz, *Logique*, Honoré et Châtelain, vol. 1, part 1, sec. 1, chap. 8, 219–23. The core of the argument is in sub-sec. 4, 222–23. In the much expanded Bousquet edition, chap. 8 occupies 459–562 of vol. 1. The core of the argument is in sub-sec. 21, 511–12.

14. Crousaz, *Logique*, Honoré and Châtelain, vol. 1, part 1, sec. 1, chap. 8, sub-sec. 4, 219–23.

15. Crousaz's strongest critiques of Leibnizian determinism are in his essays on Pope whom he attacks for being a Leibnizian determinist who misunderstands the great chain of being. (See *Examen de l'essay de M. Pope sur l'homme* [Lausanne and Amsterdam: Pierre Mortier, 1737], English trans. Elizabeth Carter [London: A. Dodd, 1739]; and *Commentaire sur la traduction en vers de M. l'abbé du Resnel de l'essai de M. Pope sur l'homme* [Genève: Pellissari, 1738], translated incompletely by Charles Forman [London: E. Curll, 1738]. A later translation, more complete, is said to be by Samuel Johnson [London: E. Cave, 1742].)

16. Jean-Pierre de Crousaz, *De Mente Humana* (Groningen: G. Elamae, 1726), 235–40.

17. Biographical information on André is not easily available. Born in 1675, he attended college at Quimper and joined the Jesuit order in 1693. He was admitted to minor orders in 1696 and taught at Alençon in the same year. In 1703, he was recalled to Paris and studied theology. Ordained a priest in 1706, he taught various subjects at Clermont and at La Flèche. There he complained—despite Descartes' claim that it was the best school in Europe—that he was in exile. In 1707, he taught at Rouen, and in 1708, at Herdily, where he first taught philosophy. In 1709, he was at Amiens, and in 1711, at Rouen again. Alençon was once more his home in 1713, and after five years there, we find him at Arras in 1718 and the next year—1719—back at Amiens. He was suspected of harbouring anti-Jesuit sentiments and documents and even of being the author of an anti-Jesuit pamphlet, an odd although not impossible charge against a Jesuit. A search of his papers turned up a manuscript of his life of Malebranche, and he landed in the Bastille. He wrote at least two letters from there, although the official prison record has not been found. Eventually, he promised to reform and was released. Immediately afterwards, he wrote on a copy of his letter of promise a rejection of it explaining that it had been written under duress—including threats of force. He spent the rest of his life going on with his work—showing no sign, ever, of any change of mind. In 1722, he was back at Amiens. He returned to Caen in 1726 and retired there in 1759. When the Jesuit order was disbanded, the local parliament voted him a pension, and he went on with his writing undisturbed. He finished his *Metaphysica* "towards Halloween" of 1760 when he was 85 years old. It remains in manuscript.

18. M. J. Carlez, *La Musique et la societé caenaise au XVIIIième siècle* (Caen: Imprimerie F. le Blanc-Hardel, 1884), 10.

19. Yves-Marie André, *Traité de l'homme selon ses differentes merveilles* (Paris: Yverdon, 1766); reprinted in Victor Cousin's edition of André's *Oeuvres philosophiques* (Paris: Charpentier, 1843).

20. André's *Discours sur la nature des idées* was originally the thirteenth discourse, 2:89–150, of the Yverdon edition of *Traité de l'homme*. (The Cousin edition has the crucial passages, 236–46, but there are omissions.)

21. See André, 241, of the Cousin edition of the *Oeuvres*; see also *Le Père André, Jésuite, Documents inédits pour servir à l'histoire philosophique religieuese et littéraire du XVIII° siècle*, ed. Antoine Charma and D. Mancel, vol. 1 (Caen: Imprimerie Lesaulnier, 1844); vol. 2 (Paris: Hachette, 1856), 1:284–87.

22. André, *Metaphysica*, page 59 of MS. 324 (in f. 24 1880 10073) in the Bibliothèque Municipale de Caen. This manuscript is written in what seems, from comparison with the numerous samples there are of his handwriting, to be André's own hand.

23. André, *Père André, Documents inédits*, 1:341. I have not been able to identify the Jesuit who wrote to André, although he seems to have been André's Provincial.

24. André, *Metaphysica*, 64–65.

25. André, *Metaphysica*, 44.

26. André, *Documents inédits*, 2:359.

27. Jean-Paul Sartre did draw this conclusion, though I know of no reason to think that he knew about André's argument.

28. André, *Metaphysica*, 110.
29. André, *Metaphysica*, 3, 4.
30. André, *Metaphysica*, 110, 111.
31. André, *Documents inédits*, 1:273–74.
32. Caen MS. 323.
33. Caen MS. 323, 453.
34. André, *Metaphysica*, 90–103.
35. André, *Metaphysica*, 90, 91.
36. André, *Metaphysica*, 99.
37. André, *Metaphysica*, 103.
38. André, *Metaphysica*, 97.
39. André, *Metaphysica*, 124.
40. André, *Metaphysica*, 125.
41. André, *Documents inédits*, 1:288–91.
42. André, *Documents inédits*, 1:288.
43. The guilt feelings need not be personal. Probably, Pascal regretted his youthful passion for the high life of Paris and his foot-dragging when his sister wanted to enter Port-Royal. But throughout his writings there is a sense that human beings, especially as they were represented by public and ecclesiastical authority in France, had tried to create their own well-ordered world. Within it, he suspected, the proper end of the human person was not taken to be the well being and glory of God, but human well being.

5. The Human Predicament and the New Skepticism

1. The "academics" derived their name from their association with the Platonic Academy. Arcesilaus, c. 315–240 B.C., is the only skeptic mentioned by name in the *Pensées* (LD 290, B 375, LL 402 says that he became a dogmatist). His name is spelled Archesilas in Pascal's manuscript.
2. Carneades, c. 213–128 B.C.
3. Pyrrho lived from c. 360–270 B.C. Virtually nothing is really known of him. It is believed that he wrote nothing, but something can be glimpsed of him through his pupil Timon of Phlius, c. 320–230 B.C. The dates of these philosophers vary widely in different reference books. There is a good recent discussion in Leo Groarke, *Greek Scepticism* (Montreal and Kingston: McGill-Queen's University Press, 1990), 85–97. Groarke emphasizes the practical concerns of Pyrrho, especially the search for the calm life. He also insists on Pyrrho's antimetaphysical stance but thinks, reasonably, that Pyrrho would not have walked over precipices. Much of what we know about the Pyrrhonists is conveniently summarized in A. A. Long's *Hellenistic Philosophy* (London: Duckworth, 1974), 75–87.
4. Groarke says, "Pyrrho himself is, like Socrates, very much a moralist" (87). Long (93–94), notes that Cicero's belief seems to clash with Diogenes Laertius, who suggests that Pyrrho believed that human behavior is (and should be) governed by convention, but the two views *might* not clash. Pyrrho may well have believed that the good life for a human is a life of calm repose and that this is furthered by not attacking convention.
5. Thomas Aquinas, *Summa Theologica*, part 1, question 79, article 4 (Turin: Typographica Pontifica, 1915), 1:514; trans. English Dominican Fathers (London: Burns, Oates, and Washburn, 1920), 4:100.
6. LD 585, B 793, LL 308.
7. Hobbes published his *Leviathan* in 1651.
8. LD 47, B 61, LL 694.
9. LD 391, B 347, LL 200.
10. See Baird, *Studies in Pascal's Ethics*.
11. See Dominique Janicaud, *La puissance du rationnel* (Paris: Gallimard, 1985), 367–72.
12. LD 390, B 72, LL 199.
13. LD 224, B 277, LL 423. By this phrase, Pascal means to call attention to a variety of intuitions that transcend mechanical reasons. Some of them are indubitably moral.

14. LD 257, B 358, LL 678 has it that an individual is neither angel nor beast, but that "he who wants to act the angel, acts the beast." LD 236, B 418, LL 121 adds that it is dangerous—though salutary—to show humans how much they resemble the beasts. One must not do so without also pointing out the greatness of humans.

15. LD 343, B 233, LL 418.

16. *Ens,* a word without which scholastic philosophy is hardly possible, did not exist as a noun in classical Latin.

17. LD 390, B 72, LL 199.

18. The occurrences of *néant* in LD 343, B 233, LL 418; LD 11, B 194, LL 427; and LD 15, B 194 bis and ter, LL 432 illustrate these two themes.

19. LD 390, B 72, LL 199.

20. In his discussion of *l'anéantissement,* Henri Gouhier tracks many uses of *néant* in Pascal (*Blaise Pascal, conversion et apologétique,* chap. 2). But the focus of his study is, as his title makes clear, on Pascal's religion.

21. Florence L. Wickelgren in *La Mothe le Vayer, sa vie et son oeuvre* (Paris: E. Droz, 1934) takes this view and argues it at length. There is a long discussion making much of La Mothe le Vayer's skepticism in René Pintard's *Le Libertinage érudit* (Geneva: Slatkine, 1983), 134–47, 178–82, 302–4, 431–32, 505–43 (this is an expanded edition of a work that first appeared in 1943). Pintard is above all concerned with religious skepticism, however, not with La Mothe le Vayer's philosophy of history.

22. Charles Chesneau, "Stoicisme et 'libertinage' dans l'oeuvre de François La Mothe le Vayer," *Revue des sciences humaines* (July–September 1954): 281–83. There is a balanced discussion of this question in Richard H. Popkin, *The History of Scepticism from Erasmus to Spinoza,* 3d ed. (Berkeley: University of California Press, 1979), 90–97, 104–6.

23. François de la Mothe le Vayer, *Petit discours chrétien de l'immortalité de l'âme* (Paris: J. Camusat, 1637).

24. François de la Mothe le Vayer, *De la vertu des payens* (Paris: F. Targa, 1642).

25. This seems to be what La Mothe le Vayer wants to convey quite late in his life in *Problèmes sceptiques* (Paris: T. Jolly, 1666). His dialogues written thirty and more years earlier convey the same impression. The *Dialogues faits a l'imitation des anciens* was first issued with 1604 as a date, Frankfurt as the alleged place of origin, the apparently imaginary J. Sarius as publisher, and the certainly imaginary Oratius Tubero as author. It was probably published in Paris c. 1630. After it but before *Problèmes sceptiques* comes the *Petit traité sceptique sur cette commune façon de parler: "n'avoir pas le sens commun"* (Paris: A. Courbé, 1646).

26. La Mothe le Vayer, *De la preuve par comparaison d'écritures.* The question that he poses is whether proof through a comparison of handwriting meets the standards of the criminal law or the lesser standards of the civil law. He thinks that criminal evidence must depend, according to the legal tradition, on documents that are evidence for themselves (a modern example would be a piece of paper currency), on the testimony of witnesses who are above reproach, or on indications that serve as premises for logical deductions. He argues that proof by comparison of handwriting does not fall into any of these categories and therefore cannot figure in criminal proof though it may be useful (but inconclusive) in other circumstances. The argument is in terms of the relative doubtfulness of handwriting tests compared to some other kinds of proof, and it draws heavily on the acceptability of a legal tradition the existence of which is established by historical methods. I have been able to consult this work only in the National Library of Canada copy, published in 1727 (Paris: J. Montelant), bound with some other legal treatises and listed under the name of the collector, "Danty, fl. 1680" (no initials given). It does not appear in the bibliography of the Bibliothèque Nationale holdings of La Mothe le Vayer's work as listed by Wickelgren in *La Mothe le Vayer, sa vie et son oeuvre* or under the author's name in the library's printed catalog, though the Bibliothèque Nationale does possess a copy, also bound with other legal treatises.

27. La Mothe le Vayer's writings on the theory and philosophy of history include *Discours de l'histoire* (Paris: J. Camusat, 1638); *La science de l'histoire avec le jugement des principaux historiens, tant anciens que modernes* (Paris: L. Billaine, 1665); and "Du peu de certitude qu'il y a dans l'histoire," in *Oeuvres de François de la Mothe le Vayer,* vol. 13 (Paris: J. Billaine, 1669), 409–48.

28. Much more study needs to be done of La Mothe le Vayer's historical theories and their place

in his thought. In the sense that history does not fit within the bounds of the propositions about which he was fully skeptical (knowledge of nature) or within the bounds of propositions that call out for committed belief (religion), history seems to have been a special problem in his mind. He tells us in "Du peu de certitude qu'il y a dans l'histoire" (*Oeuvres,* 13:409–48) that history is like a painting; the historian must make all the parts fit together coherently. At least twice (*Oeuvres,* 3:27 and 5:287) he speaks of "the laws of history." He means laws of historical writing, which require dispassion and balance, but the suggestion is that these will lead to the truth. He constantly asserts that history is not mere oratory and that the historian must always search for truth even though there are many obstacles in the form of political bias, mythology, and of course, religion. (In "Du peu de certitude qu'il y a dans l'histoire," readers are advised not to be believe what pagans say about Jews or what Christians say in disparaging Moors and Mohammedans.)

29. These figures are from Davidson and Dubé's *Concordance.*

30. Brunschvicg numbered it 434, and Chevalier 438. Here, as is so often true with other fragments, arguments have been found for widely different placings in Pascal's scheme.

31. The order I have been citing in the notes as LD and LL. Of course the principles Lafuma is using ensure that they will come together in both orderings. The point of the comparison between the assigned locations is to call attention to the contexts of the Brunschvicg and Chevalier orderings. See Note on Texts.

32. LD 47, B 61, LL 694.

33. LD 289, B 378, LL 518.

34. LD 296, B 51, LL 886.

35. LD 355, B 268, LL 170.

36. LD 290, B 375, LL 520.

37. Augustine's work is translated as *Against the Academicians* by Mary Patricia Garvey (Milwaukee: Marquette University Press, 1957).

38. LD 290, B 375, LL 520.

39. LD 746, B 790, LL 940.

40. LD 171, B 299, LL 81.

41. LD 171, B 299, LL 81.

42. The claim that we have an image of truth but "possess" only lies is made in LD 246, B 434, LL 131. The claim that we have an idea of truth invincible to Pyrrhonism is in LD 287, B 395, LL 406.

43. LD 298, B 385, LL 905.

44. LD 27, B 184, LL 4.

45. LD 295, B 432, LL 691.

46. LD 294, B 391, LL 658.

47. LD 402, B 435, LL 208. It *may* be significant that in this passage Pascal speaks specifically of "academicians" and not of Pyrrhonists.

48. LD 293, B 394, LL 619.

49. LD 44, B 373, LL 532.

50. LD 364, B 256, LL 179.

51. John Henry Newman, *An Essay in Aid of a Grammar of Assent* (1870; New York: Doubleday, 1955).

52. Pascal seems to have grasped the issue in his repeated insistence on the concept of infinity, though he did not spell it out. To be precise, in the language with which we communicate with a machine, we can express one more propositional attitude than it can, for it has some program, which we can readily find, without which it would not be functioning. This implies one proposition that it cannot reject. Of course, this holds true only in a certain universe of discourse. Outside this universe of discourse we too may be programmed in ways that simply do not show in our imaginary contest with the machine. Perhaps, indeed, we could design another kind of computer that had this kind of logical independence in the universe of discourse within which it could communicate with itself. But the machine could not continue to reject every proposition in infinitely many universes of discourse, because it is still, like Pascal's machine, a finite discrete state device. Pascal insists that it is our link with the infinite that matters.

53. This remains so, for it probable that A. M. Turing's account of the general properties of

calculating machines, for instance, is more certain than our knowledge of how any particular computer works. (See A. M. Turing, "Computing Machinery and Intelligence," *Mind*, n.s., 59 [1950]; reprinted in Alan Ross Anderson, ed., *Minds and Machines* [Englewood Cliffs, N.J.: Prentice Hall, 1964].)

54. See especially LD 577, B 786, LL 300; LD 586, B 797, LL 309; LD 487, B 679, LL 253; LD 380, B 547, LL 89; LD 406, B 528, LL 212.

55. LD 741, B 785, LL 946.

56. Here, in LD 741, B 785, LL 946, somewhat exceptionally, Pascal uses *personnes* and not *hommes*, perhaps to be sure that no one misses the universality intended.

57. LD 98, B 390, LL 896.

58. LD 878, B 843, LL 840.

59. LD 11, B 194, LL 427.

60. LD 11, B 194, LL 427.

61. LD 219, B 349, LL 115.

62. I say "a" physical order because nothing Pascal says suggests that our future life, if there is one, must be here on earth or in what we think of as the present physical universe, and LD 344, B 231, LL 420 suggests that there are infinitely more things in the physical world than we know about.

63. Human history has shown, alas, the price one might pay for speculations about the answers to such questions. The deaths of millions of Jews owes something to the false belief that this happened because the Jews were wicked and some of the Gentiles were particularly deserving.

64. LD 11, B 194, LL 427 suggests that very many human beings are in peril of damnation. The nearest Pascal comes to "universalism" is in LD 349, B 239, LL 748, where he suggests that everyone may hope for salvation. Of course, at most, almost everyone could be saved because, presumably, God can do nothing about the sinner who refuses every offer of salvation, unless he turns such sinners into machines that have no free will. If he does turn them into machines, we are entitled to claim that they are no longer human souls.

65. Martin de Barcos was born in 1600 and died in 1678. He was the nephew of Duvergier de Hauranne, Abbé of St. Cyran. (He eventually acquired the ecclesiastical office of his uncle and is also, sometimes, confusingly, referred to as "St. Cyran" or "M. de St. Cyran.")

66. Martin de Barcos, *Exposition de la foi Catholique touchant la grace et la prédestination* (Mons: Gaspard Migeot, 1696), 273. Lucien Goldmann quotes it in *Le Dieu caché*, 330; *The Hidden God*, trans. Thody (London), 297–98. Goldmann quotes from the 1700 edition titled *Exposition de la foi de l'Eglise romaine concernant la grace et la prédestination*, published in Cologne by P. Marteau. (The quotation is on 275–76 of the Marteau edition—an edition that is identical in nearly all respects with the Migeot edition.)

67. Thody's translation of Goldmann, *Le Dieu caché*.

68. Goldmann, *Le Dieu caché; The Hidden God*, trans. Thody. The reference is to chapter 7 in both editions, especially 157–84 of the French and 144–62 of the English (London).

69. Antoine Arnauld and Pierre Nicole, *La Logique ou l'art de penser* (Paris: Flammarion, 1970). This standard modern edition is taken from the 5th ed. (Paris: Guillaume Desprez, 1683). There are earlier editions from 1662.

70. Martin de Barcos, *Les sentimens de M. de St. Cyran sur l'oraison mentale* (Anvers [Antwerp]: la veuve Jean Jacob, 1696). (This book was also published in the same year by Pierre Du Marteau in Cologne under the title *Les sentimens de l'abbé Philérème sur l'oraison mentale*.)

71. Jean Orcibal, *Port-Royal entre le miracle et l'obéissance* (Paris: Desclée de Brouwer, 1957), 27. Despite his association of Barcos with "anti-intellectualism," Orcibal is at pains to associate him with various strands of neo-Platonism.

72. The last thirty pages of *Les Sentimens*, Antwerp edition, depart from the dialogue and are a commentary on a theology textbook.

73. Barcos, *Les Sentimens*, Antwerp ed., 1–2.

74. Barcos, *Les Sentimens*, Antwerp ed., 34.

75. Barcos, *Les Sentimens*, Antwerp ed., 7.

76. Louis Cognet, "Le Jugement de Port-Royal sur Pascal," *Cahiers de Royaumont, Philosophie, No.1: Blaise Pascal: l'homme et l'oeuvre*, 1956, 11–30.

77. Goldmann, *Le Dieu caché*, 175; *The Hidden God*, trans. Thody (London), 156–57.

78. The quotation is from Pascal, *Oeuvres*, ed. Mesnard, 3:722; ed. Chevalier, 1044. Chevalier

used it as the concluding paragraph of the treatise. Jean Mesnard, in his chronological reconstruction, has placed it near the beginning of what he takes to be the second part. See Pascal, *Oeuvres,* ed. Mesnard, 3: 487–799; ed. Chevalier, 947–1044. So far as we can tell, the manuscript was left unfinished. We are assured by Louis Périer, our best source going back to Pascal's time, that it is genuine, though what we have is not actually the original in Pascal's handwriting.

79. Pascal, *Oeuvres,* ed. Mesnard, 3:782–83; ed. Chevalier, 949–51.

80. The manuscript in the Bibliothèque Nationale in Paris, fr. 10576, fos 11r–17v, consists of 143 sheets headed "Extrait [par Rapin] dix-huit tomes in folio, sur l'affaire des jansénistes, qui sont au St Office à Rome." A portion of them appears in Lucien Ceyssens, *Sources relatives aux débuts du jansénisme et de l'antijansénisme,* app. 2 (Louvain: Publications Universitaires, 1957), 644–59. Very many of Rapin's reflections on the Jansenists have been collected and appear in *Mémoires du P. René Rapin sur l'Église et la société, la cour, la ville et le jansénisme,* 3 vols. (Lyon and Paris: Emmanuel Vitte, 1865; reprint, Farnborough, England: Gregg International, 1972).

81. René Rapin, *L'Importance du salut* (Paris: Sebastien Mabre-Cramoisy, 1675), 195–218.

82. Rapin, *Mémoires du P. René Rapin,* 1:214.

83. Rapin, *Mémoires du P. René Rapin,* 1:361, 455.

84. LD 98, B 390, LL 896.

85. René Rapin, *L'Esprit du Christianisme* (Paris: Sebastien Mabre-Cramoisy, 1672); 2d ed. (1674).

86. In the works I have cited, *L'Importance du salut* and *L'Esprit du Christianisme,* as well as in the related *La Perfection du Christianisme* (Paris: Sebastien Mabre-Cramoisy, 1673), the vast majority of citations are from Scripture, mainly from the New Testament. Augustine is not infrequently mentioned. St. Anselm, St. Bernard, St. Jerome, and Thomas à Kempis appear as well. Indeed, Rapin concentrates on texts the Jansenists would have found attractive. The metaphysical background is not easy to identify, though Rapin's insistence on the conditions of the ordinary, commonsense world is more Aristotelian than Platonic. He insists, interestingly, on the importance of the fact that Jesus came as an infant with the limitations that that implies in the natural world (*La Perfection du Christianisme,* chap. 5, 45–61). Throughout his work, however, it is supposed that the world has a constant order and that God has reasonable and constant aims.

87. Indeed, Rapin's *Instructions pour l'histoire* (Paris: S. Mabre-Cramoisy, 1677) should be compared with La Mothe le Vayer's critique of history. Rapin's *La Comparaison de Platon et d'Aristote* (Paris: C. Babin, 1671) deals with his views about the philosophy of classical antiquity in relation to the Church fathers and Christian doctrine. A careful study of the ways in which history and tradition are used by Rapin and La Mothe le Vayer would help to clarify their views of the trade-off between doubt and belief and suggest avenues for both skeptics and believers. It might also tell us something about the roots of historicism. La Mothe le Vayer and Rapin moved in the same circles in Paris. The differences between them are subtle, for they make use of much the same literary and historical traditions.

88. See especially Malebranche's *Entretien d'un philosophe chrétien et chinois,* in *Oeuvres complètes,* vol. 15, ed. A. Robinet (Paris: J. Vrin, 1958).

WORKS CITED

André, Yves-Marie. *Essai sur le beau*. Paris: H. L. et J. Guérin, 1741; J. P. du Halde, 1744. Ed. Jean-Henri Samuel Formey. Amsterdam: J. H. Schneider, 1759.

———. *Metaphysica*. MS. 324. Bibliothèque Municipale de Caen.

———. Notebooks (extracts from Descartes and Malebranche with notes). MS. 323. Bibliothèque Municipale de Caen.

———. *Oeuvres philosophiques*. Ed. Victor Cousin. Paris: Charpentier, 1843.

———. *Le Père André, Jésuite, Documents inédits pour servir à l'histoire philosophique religieuese et littéraire du XVIIIe siècle*. Ed. Antoine Charma and D. Mancel. Vol. 1. Caen: Imprimerie Lesaulnier, 1844. Vol. 2. Paris: Hachette, 1856.

———. *Traité de l'homme selon ses differentes merveilles*. 2 vols. Paris: Yverdon, 1766.

———. *La Vie du P. Malebranche, prêtre de l'oratoire, avec l'histoire de ses ouvrages*. Paris: Ingold, 1886.

Aquinas, Thomas, Saint. *Opera Omnia*. Leonine edition. 15 vols. to date. Rome: 1892-present.

———. *Summa Theologica*. 6 vols. Turin: Typographia Pontifica, 1915. Trans. English Dominican Fathers. 22 vols. London: Burns, Oates and Washbourne, 1920.

Arnauld, Antoine, and Pierre Nicole. *La Logique ou l'art de penser*. Paris: Flammarion, 1970. From the 5th ed. Paris: Guillaume Desprez, 1683. There are earlier editions from 1662.

Arnold, Keith. "Pascal's Great Experiment." *Dialogue* 28 (1989): 401–15.

Arnold, Matthew. *St. Paul and Protestantism*. London: Smith, Elder, 1870. Included in *Prose Works of Matthew Arnold*, ed. R. H. Super. Ann Arbor: University of Michigan Press, 1968.

Augustine, Aurelius, Saint. *Contra Academicos*. Trans. as *Against the Academicians*, by Mary Patricia Garvey. Milwaukee: Marquette University Press, 1957.

Baird, A. W. S. *Studies in Pascal's Ethics*. The Hague: Martinus Nijhoff, 1975.

Barcos, Martin de. *Correspondance de Martin de Barcos*. Ed. Lucien Goldmann. Paris: Presses Universitaires de France, 1956.

———. *Exposition de la foi Catholique touchant la grace et la prédestination*. Mons: Gaspard Migeot, 1696. Republished as *Exposition de la foi de l'Eglise romaine concernant la grace et la prédestination*. Cologne: P. Marteau, 1700. The Migeot and Marteau editions are identical in nearly all respects.

———. *Les sentimens de M. de St. Cyran sur l'oraison mentale*. Anvers [Antwerp]: la veuve Jean Jacob, 1696. (Also published in the same year by Pierre Du Marteau in Cologne under the title *Les sentimens de l'abbé Philérème sur l'oraison mentale*.)

Bérulle, Pierre de. *Discours de l'éstat et des grandeurs de Jésus*. Paris: A. Estiene, 1623.

———. *Oeuvres de Cardinal Bérulle*. Ed. François Bourgoing. Paris: Antoine Estiene and Sebastien Huré, 1644.

Brunschvicg, Léon. *Blaise Pascal*. Paris: Rieder, 1932.

Carlez, M. J. *La Musique et la societé caenaise au XVIIIième siècle*. Caen: Imprimerie F. le Blanc-Hardel, 1884.

Ceyssens, Lucien. *Sources relatives aux débuts du jansénisme et de l'antijansénisme*. Louvain: Publications Universitaires, 1957.

Chateaubriand, François René de. *Oeuvres*. 12 vols. Paris: Garnier, 1859.

Chesneau, Charles [also known as Julien-Eymard d'Angers]. *Le Père Yves de Paris et son temps*. 2 vols. Paris: Societé de l'Histoire Ecclésiastique de la France, 1946.

————. "Stoicisme et 'libertinage' dans l'oeuvre de François La Mothe le Vayer." *Revue des sciences humaines* (July–September 1954): 281–83.

Chevalier, Jacques. *Pascal*. Paris: Plon, 1923.

Chibaudel, Pierre. "Sur le fragment des trois ordres de Pascal." *Archives de philosophie* 53 (1990): 631–45.

Cognet, Louis. "Le Jugement de Port-Royal sur Pascal." *Cahiers de Royaumont, Philosophie, No.1: Blaise Pascal: l'homme et l'oeuvre*, 1956.

Crousaz, Jean-Pierre de. *Commentaire sur la traduction en vers de M. l'abbé du Resnel de l'essai de M. Pope sur l'homme*. Genève: Pellissari, 1738. Trans. Charles Forman. London: E. Curll, 1738 (incomplete). Trans. ascribed to Samuel Johnson. London: E. Cave, 1742.

————. *Examen de l'essay de M. Pope sur l'homme*. Lausanne and Amsterdam: Pierre Mortier, 1737. Trans. Elizabeth Carter. London: A. Dodd, 1739.

————. *Examen du pyrrhonisme ancien et moderne*. The Hague: Pierre de Hondt, 1733.

————. *Logique, abrégé*. Amsterdam: Z. Châtelain, 1737.

————. *La Logique ou système de reflexions*. 3 vols. Amsterdam: Honoré et Châtelain, 1720, 6 vols. Lausanne and Geneva: Bousquet, 1741.

————. *De Mente Humana*. Groningen: G. Elamae, 1726.

————. *Traité du beau*. Amsterdam: F. L. Honoré, 1715; Paris: Fayard, 1985.

Dalton, Peter C. "Pascal's Wager, the First Argument." *International Journal for the Philosophy of Religion* 7 (1976): 346–68.

————. "Pascal's Wager, the Second Argument." *Southern Journal of Philosophy* 13 (1975): 31–46.

Davidson, Hugh M., and Pierre H. Dubé. *Concordance to Pascal's Pensées*. Ithaca: Cornell University Press, 1975.

Davis, Stephen T. "Pascal on Self-Caused Belief." *Religious Studies* 27 (1991): 27–37.

Descartes, René. *Oeuvres*. Ed. Charles Adam and Paul Tannery. Revised under the direction of the Centre Nationale de la Recherche Scientifique. Paris: J. Vrin, 1964–75.

————. *Oeuvres philosophiques*. Ed. Ferdinand Alquié. Paris: Garnier, 1973.

Eddington, Sir Arthur. *The Nature of the Physical Universe*. Cambridge: The University Press, 1927, 1930.

Eustachius a Sancto Paulo. *Exercices spirituels contenant plusieurs méditations*. Paris: M. du Puis, 1630.

————. *Summa Philosophiae Quadrapartita*. Paris: C. Chastellain, 1609 (*Chastellain* is spelled *Chastelain* in the 1613 edition). Cambridge: Roger Daniels, 1640.

————. *Summa Theologiae Tripartita*. Paris: Carolus Chastelain (with one l), 1613–16.

Goldmann, Lucien. *Le Dieu caché*. Paris: Gallimard, 1955. Trans. Philip Thody as *The Hidden God*. London: Routledge & Kegan Paul; New York: Humanities Press, 1964.

Gouhier, Henri. *Blaise Pascal, Commentaire*. Paris: J. Vrin, 1966, 1984.

————. *Blaise Pascal, conversion et apologétique*. Paris: J. Vrin, 1986.

Groarke, Leo. *Greek Scepticism*. Montreal and Kingston: McGill-Queen's University Press, 1990.

Hacking, Ian. "The Logic of Pascal's Wager." *American Philosophical Quarterly* 9 (1972): 186–92.

Hobbes, Thomas. *Leviathan*. London: Andrew Cooke, 1651, Ed. Michael Oakeshott. Oxford: Basil Blackwell, 1955.

Hurlbutt, Robert H., III. *Hume, Newton, and the Design Argument*. Lincoln: University of Nebraska Press, 1965.

Janicaud, Dominique. *La puissance du rationnel*. Paris: Gallimard, 1985.

Kant, Immanuel. *Critique of Practical Reason* (1788). Trans. Lewis White Beck. New York: Liberal Arts Press, 1956.

Lachelier, Jules. "Notes on the *Pari* de Pascal." In *The Philosophy of Jules Lachelier*, ed. and trans. Edward G. Ballard, 97–110. The Hague: Martinus Nijhoff, 1960.

La Mothe le Vayer, François de. *De la preuve par comparaison d'écritures*. Paris: J. Montelant, 1727.

———. *De la vertu des payens*. Paris: F. Targa, 1642.

———. *Dialogues faits à l'imitation des anciens*. By Oratius Tubero [François de la Mothe le Vayer]. N.p. Paris: c. 1630. Earliest known copy carries the date 1604 and the imprint Frankfurt: J. Sarius, but these are believed to be spurious. (Earliest version entitled *Quatre dialogues*, later *Cinq dialogues*, etc.)

———. *Discours de l'histoire*. Paris: J. Camusat, 1638.

———. *Oeuvres de François de la Mothe le Vayer*. 15 vols. Paris: L. Billaine, 1669.

———. *Petit discours chrétien de l'immortalité de l'âme*. Paris: J. Camusat, 1637.

———. *Petit traité sceptique sur cette commune façon de parler: "n'avoir pas le sens commun."* Paris: A. Courbé, 1646.

———. *Problèmes sceptiques*. Paris: T. Jolly, 1666.

———. *La science de l'histoire avec le jugement des principaux historiens, tant anciens que modernes*. Paris: L. Billaine, 1665.

Landsberg, P. T. "Gambling on God." *Mind*, n.s. 80 (1971): 100–104.

Locke, John. *An Essay Concerning Human Understanding*. London 1690. 4th ed. Awnsham and John Churchil, 1700. This edition is the source of the standard modern edition. Ed. Peter H. Nidditch. Oxford: The Clarendon Press, 1975.

———. *An Examination of P. Malebranche's Opinion of seeing all Things in God*. In *Posthumous Works of Mr. John Locke*. London: W. B. for A. and J. Churchill, 1706.

———. *Remarks upon some of Mr. Norris's Books, wherein he asserts P. Malebranche's Opinion of seeing all Things in God*. In *A Collection of several Pieces of Mr. John Locke*. London: J. Bettesworth for R. Franklin, 1720.

Long, A. A. *Hellenistic Philosophy*. London: Duckworth, 1974.

Lønning, Per. *Cet effrayant pari*. Paris: J. Vrin, 1980.

Malebranche, Nicolas. *Entretien d'un philosophe chrétien et chinois*. In *Oeuvres complètes*. Vol. 15. Ed A. Robinet. Paris: J. Vrin, 1958.

Manuel, Frank E. *A Portrait of Isaac Newton*. London: Frederick Muller, 1980.

———. *The Religion of Isaac Newton*. Oxford: The Clarendon Press, 1974.

Mossé-Bastide, Rose-Marie. *Bergson et Plotin*. Paris: Presses Universitaires de France, 1959.

Nadler, Steven M. *Arnauld and the Cartesian Philosophy of Ideas*. Princeton: Princeton University Press, 1989.

Newman, John Henry. *An Essay in Aid of a Grammar of Assent*, 1870. Reprint. New York: Doubleday, 1955.

Orcibal, Jean. *Duvergier de Hauranne, abbé de Saint-Cyran et son temps*. 2 vols. Paris: J. Vrin, 1947.

———. *Port-Royal entre le miracle et l'obéissance*. Paris: Desclée de Brouwer, 1957.

Pascal, Blaise. *Lettres Provinciales*. Paris: 1656 as a series of pamphlets; collected Cologne: Pierre de la Vallée, 1657. Ed. Jean Steinmann. Paris: Armand Colin, 1962 (bound with the response of Gabriel Daniel, S. J.).

———. *Oeuvres complètes*. Ed. Jacques Chevalier. Paris: Gallimard, Pléiade, 1954.

————. *Oeuvres complètes*. Ed. Jean Mesnard. 3 vols. Paris: Desclée de Brouwer, 1964, 1970, 1991.

————. *Pensées*. Paris: Guillaume Desprez, 1669.

————. *Pensées*. Facsimile editions. Ed. Léon Brunschvicg. Paris: Hachette, 1905. Ed. Louis Lafuma. Paris: Les Librairies Associées, 1962.

————. *Pensées*. Ed. G. Michaut. Fribourg, Switzerland: The University Press, 1896.

————. *Pensées*. Ed. Jacques Chevalier. 2 vols. Paris: Gabalda, 1925.

————. *Pensées*. Ed. Léon Brunschvicg. 3 vols. Paris: Hachette, 1904. With new introduction by Robert Garric. Paris: Hachette, 1950.

————. *Pensées*. Ed. Louis Lafuma. 2 vols. Paris: Delmas, 1948. Rev. (2 vols. in 1). 1952, 1960.

————. *Pensées*. Ed. Louis Lafuma. 3 vols. Paris: Editions du Luxembourg, 1951. 2d ed. 1952. Rev. 1 vol. Paris: Seuil, 1963 (text with same numbers as 1951 ed. but without critical apparatus).

————. *Pensées*. Ed. Zacharie Tourneur. "edition paléographique." Transcribes Bibliothèque Nationale MS. 9202. Paris: J. Vrin, 1942.

————. *Pensées*. Ed. and trans. H. F. Stewart. London: Routledge & Kegan Paul, 1950.

————. *Pensées*. Trans. A. J. Krailsheimer. Harmondsworth, Middlesex: Penguin, 1966.

————. *Pensées*. Trans. John Warrington. Everyman No. 874. London: Dent, 1960.

Penelhum, Terence. *God and Skepticism*. Dordrecht: D. Reidel, 1983.

————. "Pascal's Wager." *Journal of Religion* 44 (1964): 201–9.

Pintard, René. *Le Libertinage érudit*. Geneva: Slatkine, 1983 (expansion of 1943 edition).

Popkin, Richard H. *The History of Scepticism from Erasmus to Spinoza*. 3rd ed. Berkeley: University of California Press, 1979.

Pugh, Anthony R. *The Composition of Pascal's Apologia*. Toronto: The University Press, 1984.

Rapin, René. *La Comparaison de Platon et d'Aristote*. Paris: C. Babin, 1671.

————. *L'Esprit du Christianisme*. Paris: Sebastien Mabre-Cramoisy, 1672. 2d ed. 1674.

————. *"Extrait [par Rapin] des dix-huit tomes en folio, sur l'affaire des jansénistes, qui sont au St Office à Rome."* MS. fr. 10576, fos 11r–17v. Bibliothèque Nationale, Paris. (A portion appears in Ceyssens, *Sources relatives aux débuts du jansénisme et de l'antijansénisme*.)

————. *L'Importance du salut*. Paris: Sebastien Mabre-Cramoisy, 1675.

————. *Instructions pour l'histoire*. Paris: Sebastien Mabre-Cramoisy, 1677.

————. *Mémoires du P. René Rapin sur l'Église et la société, la cour, la ville et le jansénisme*. 3 vols. Lyon and Paris: Emmanuel Vitte, 1865. Reprint. Farnborough, England: Gregg International, 1972.

————. *La Perfection du Christianisme*. Paris: Sebastien Mabre-Cramoisy, 1673.

Rescher, Nicholas. *Pascal's Wager*. Notre Dame: Notre Dame University Press, 1985.

Rotrou, Jean de. *Le Véritable Saint Genest*. Paris: Toussainct Quinet, 1647; Sand, for the Comédie Française, 1988.

Tillotson, John. *The Wisdom of Being Religious*. London: S. Gellibrand, 1664.

Turing, A. M. "Computing Machinery and Intelligence." *Mind*, n.s. 59 (1950). Reprinted in Alan Ross Anderson, ed. *Minds and Machines*. Englewood Cliffs, N.J: Prentice Hall, 1964.

Watson, Richard A. *The Breakdown of Cartesian Metaphysics*. Incorporates a revised version of *The Downfall of Cartesianism*. New York: Humanities Press, 1987.

Wickelgren, Florence L. *La Mothe le Vayer, sa vie et son oeuvre*. Paris: E. Droz, 1934.

Yves de Paris. *L'Agent de Dieu dans le monde*. Paris: Thierry, 1656.

————. *De l'indifférence*. Paris: Thierry, 1638. Reprint. Paris: Belles-Lettres, 1966.

————. *Digestium Sapientiae*. Vol. 1. Paris: Thierry, 1648, Vol. 2. 1654.

————. *La Théologie naturelle ou les premières véritez de foy eclaircies par raisons sensibles et moralles*. 4 vols. Paris: Nicolas Buon, 1633, 1640.

————. *Très-humbles remonstrances presentées à la reine contre les nouvelles doctrines de ce temps*. Paris, 1644.

INDEX

Academics: how different from Pyr-
rhonists, 53; how named, 95n.1; their
claims to universal doubt, 60
Adam and Eve, 79
Adventitious ideas. *See* Ideas
Aesthetics: and innate ideas, 51. *See also*
André, Yves-Marie; Crousaz, Jean-
Pierre de
Alexander, Samuel, 93n.1
André, Yves-Marie, xi, xii, 17, 25, 44,
47, 50–59, 83; and Descartes and
Malebranche, 54; on God and ideas,
52; his life, 94n.17; and incom-
pleteness of the world, 56; on original-
ity of factitious ideas, 58
Anéantissement: meaning of, 96n.20
Animal nature, 16
Annat, François, 80
Aquinas, Thomas, Saint: and form of the
good, 61
Arcesilaus (Archesilas), 66–67
Arguments: Pascal's, 3, 12, 14; Pascal-
ian-Platonist, 68
Aristotelianism and scientific knowledge,
18
Arnauld, Angélique, 11, 77
Arnauld, Antoine, 18, 47, 77, 93n.3
Arnold, Keith, 88n.28
Arnold, Matthew, 8
Augustine, Saint, 16, 67, 79
Augustinian neo-Platonism, xi, 2, 35

Baird, A. W. S., 33, 36, 62
Barcos, Martin de, 76–80; consistency of
his theology, 77; doubts *human* reason, 77; and God's justice, 76; and
God's mercy, 76; his God a good
bet?, 82; his life, 98n.65; knows the
"God within," 78; not anti-intellectual,

77; other-worldliness of, 79; thinks of
God as Truth and Justice, 78
Bayle, Pierre: why opposed by Crousaz,
47
Beatitude, 39
Beauty: involved with goodness and
truth, 40; and knowledge of God, 50;
and virtue (Crousaz's theory of), 47–
50
Belief: and acting, 66; animal faith and,
66; best bet if there are only two options, 4; and certainty that one is
doubting, 53; classical skeptic had no
strong predilection for, 29; Descartes
useless as source for, 61; and doubt,
trade-off between, 60–62; fideistic,
13; God, disturbed by lack of?, 1;
grounds for withholding, 60; improves
the mind in certain circumstances, 8;
and the Incarnation, 17; intellectual,
9; La Mothe le Vayer's (logical question of), 63–64; logic does not compel, 72; metaphysical, 10; not simply
a mental state, 61; our natures lead us
into, 13; in reality of the external
world, 71; religious foundation for,
xii; skeptical preference for doubt
over, 60; trade-off with doubt, 9; withholding, 10, 60. *See also* Doubt;
Knowledge; Libertines; Pyrrhonism;
Skepticism
Bergson, Henri, 93n.1
Berkeley, George, 63
Bérulle, Pierre de, xi, 7, 12, 14; on emanations of God, 16; his idea of *infini
rien,* 16; mysticism of, 15–16; opti-
mism of, 16; and science, 15–16; support of Copernicus, 61
Bets, good: conditions for, 71–72; three
senses of, 2

107

Born in Canada and educated there and in England, Leslie Armour holds a doctorate from the University of London and has taught at various universities in the United States and Canada. He is now professor of philosophy at the University of Ottawa. His books include *The Rational and the Real*, *Logic and Reality*, *The Concept of Truth*, *The Idea of Canada and the Crisis of Community*, and *Being and Idea*, as well as *The Faces of Reason* (written with Elizabeth Trott) and *The Conceptualization of the Inner Life* (written with Edward T. Bartlett III).